MINIMUS SECU

Moving on in Latin
Teacher's Resource Book

Barbara Bell

Joint Association of Classical Teachers

Illustrated by **Helen Forte**

CAMBRIDGE
UNIVERSITY PRESS

PUBLISHED BY THE PRESS SYNDICATE OF THE UNIVERSITY OF CAMBRIDGE
The Pitt Building, Trumpington Street, Cambridge, United Kingdom

CAMBRIDGE UNIVERSITY PRESS
The Edinburgh Building, Cambridge CB2 2RU, UK
40 West 20th Street, New York, NY 10011-4211, USA
477 Williamstown Road, Port Melbourne, VIC 3207, Australia
Ruiz de Alarcón 13, 28014 Madrid, Spain
Dock House, The Waterfront, Cape Town 8001, South Africa

http://www.cambridge.org

First published 2004
Reprinted 2004

Printed in the United Kingdom at the University Press, Cambridge

Typefaces Macra Palatino, Scala sans and Tempus *System* QuarkXPress®

A catalogue record for this book is available from the British Library

ISBN 0 521 75546 8 paperback

Produced by Kamae Design, Oxford
Design by Angela Ashton
Illustrations by Helen Forte

Contents

Introduction

Minimus secundus is designed as a sequel to *Minimus: Starting out in Latin*, which was published in 1999. Those who have already used that book will be familiar with the main characters, a Roman family who actually lived at Vindolanda. Much of this introduction is aimed at teachers who have not used *Minimus* before and for whom the cheeky mouse – and indeed Latin – may be something of a novelty.

There is no need to be a Classical scholar to use these two books; *Minimus* is taught by some who have never studied Latin at all but who are learning alongside their pupils. With this in mind, all the Latin passages are translated and the answers to all the exercises are given in this Teacher's Resource Book.

Teachers who are anxious about how to pronounce Latin may find the accompanying audio cassette helpful. *Minimus* is part of a campaign to promote the learning of Latin amongst our youngest children (the *Primary Latin Project*). Those proposing to teach it may also wish to make use of the associated training days and support materials. Further details are available from the author of *Minimus* and director of the *Primary Latin Project*: Mrs Barbara Bell, 82 Swiss Drive, Ashton, Bristol BS3 2RW, England. E-mail: bmbellmini@aol.com

You can also visit the *Minimus* website: www.minimus-etc.co.uk

The activities described in these teaching notes are merely suggestions; how much use you make of them will depend on the age and ability of your pupils and the time available for teaching. The core material in each chapter is:

- the picture stories;
- grasp the grammar;
- vocabulary to be learnt (listed in this Teacher's Resource Book).

The target age range for this book is approximately 10–13, for pupils in both preparatory and state schools. Wherever possible, links have been made with the *National Literacy Strategy* (NLS) as some head teachers have adapted *Minimus* for use within the government's Literacy Hour.

Background information

In *Minimus*, pupils followed the fortunes of a real family who lived in the Roman camp at Vindolanda (near Hexham, south of Hadrian's Wall) at the beginning of the second century AD. We know of the family's existence from the famous Vindolanda writing tablets. Many of these tablets are now displayed in the British Museum in London, where in 2002 they were voted the most important British treasures in the collection. The father of the family is Flavius Cerialis, the prefect of the camp. He commanded the ninth cohort of Batavians (from the Netherlands). His wife is Sulpicia Lepidina and we know that they had three children. The names and ages of the children are not known but in the first book they were envisaged as being about three, 13 and 16. The family had three slaves – the Greek Corinthus, the Celtic Candidus and the attractive local slave girl, Pandora. Other key members of the group are the fictitious Minimus, the family's pet mouse, and his arch-enemy, the cat Vibrissa ('Whiskers').

In *Minimus secundus*, time has moved on five years. It is now the summer of AD 105. Flavius Cerialis (known as Flavius) has been the prefect of the camp for six years, an unusual double posting. He is now 45 and is leaving the Roman army. He has accepted a post in the imperial civil service in Eboracum (York). Accompanying him to York will be his wife Lepidina, now 37, and their younger son Rufus who is now eight.

Their three slaves will also go with them. The elder son, Iulius, is now 18 and is eager to join the Roman army. He will be leaving for Dacia (modern Romania) to serve under Trajan in his second Dacian War. Their daughter Flavia is now 21 and is married to the commanding officer at Cataractonium (Catterick). Vibrissa is now a much older cat and even more sluggish than in the first book but Minimus is a supermouse, who has lived longer than anyone expected. . .

General aims of this book

1 By following the fortunes of this family, pupils will be able to understand more of what life was like in Britain under the Romans. The first two chapters focus on the end of the family's time at Vindolanda. Chapter 3 covers their move to York and the remaining chapters deal with the family's new life in York. The 12 chapters follow the 12 months of the year. The course is intended to complement work in history lessons, where primary pupils usually study the Roman invasion of Britain.

2 *Minimus secundus* enables pupils to move on in Latin. They will meet their first past tense (the imperfect, e.g. **portābam** 'I was carrying') and other forms of the verb. Case structure is still limited to the nominative and the accusative. If the pupils are fortunate enough to go on to study Latin at secondary school, they will not have learnt enough Latin for this to present a serious problem. On the contrary, it is hoped that the grammatical structures and vocabulary that they meet in this book will ease the transition to other Latin courses, and indeed to the learning of modern foreign languages.

3 It is a key aim of both *Minimus* books to teach English grammar through simple Latin. Work on parts of speech, vocabulary patterns, links with other languages, derivations, prefixes and suffixes should therefore be integral to any *Minimus* lesson. Since two thirds of all the words we use in English are derived from either Latin or Classical Greek, pupils will find Latin extremely useful in their understanding of English. Many of the volunteer teachers of *Minimus* speak with gratitude of the usefulness of the Latin that they studied at school.

4 Above all, pupils should have fun as they identify with the characters and follow their adventures. There are endless opportunities for cross-curricular activities. It is hoped that time may be found for some of these activities, even in a lunch-time or after-school club.

Course structure

Each chapter contains the following elements:

PICTURE STORY
This introduces the subject matter and language for the chapter.

WORDS TO HELP
This section lists new vocabulary from the picture story. The words are arranged according to parts of speech. Pupils may take time to get used to this but the long-term benefits of understanding parts of speech will more than compensate for some initial slowness in finding the right word. It is deliberate policy not to explain every new word in this section. Pupils should be guided to guess intelligently before looking up unfamiliar words in the glossary at the back of the book.

GRASP THE GRAMMAR
This section introduces and explains grammatical concepts. It is usually followed by reinforcement activities.

ROMAN REPORT
This section contains information about Roman life. It is sometimes followed by points for discussion. The illustrations and photographs provide many opportunities for valuable oral work.

LATIN ROOTS
This section introduces derivatives from Latin words.

MYTHOLOGY
A myth or story, told in English.

WORDS TO REMEMBER

This section reinforces key vocabulary from the chapter. In *Minimus secundus* this is to be found in the Teacher's Resource Book (see pages 93–95).

Reading aloud

It is highly desirable for pupils to read their Latin aloud, if time permits. Here are some hints on Latin pronunciation:

- There are no silent letters in Latin. Pronounce every letter.
- There was no letter 'J' in the Roman alphabet: hence Iulius (pronounced 'Youlius').
- Evidence suggests that the Romans in Italy, and in Britain at this period, pronounced the letter 'v' as a 'w'. So the name of our cat is 'Wibrissa'!
- Romans stressed both letters in double consonants. So the double 's' in Vibrissa suggests the hissing sound of the cat.
- The letter 'c' is always hard, as in 'cat'.

Certain vowels have horizontal lines above them: these are known as *macra* (from the Greek word *makros* meaning 'long'). They are not accents and pupils should not include them when writing Latin. Macra are a guide to pronunciation and indicate long vowels. Here are some examples from the first picture story (page 6): Lepidīna (Lepid**ee**na), spectā ('a' as in **a**rt), incēdunt ('e' as in d**ay**).

Learning vocabulary

The main difficulty is for pupils to remember vocabulary from week to week, especially if they have no official homework time. Here are some suggestions to aid vocabulary learning.

- Teachers should stress that pupils do not need to remember every word they meet. The key words are listed at the end of each chapter in the 'Words to remember' section of these teaching notes. They are also provided on photocopiable sheets on pages 93–95.
- Pupils will benefit from recapping these key words in some way in every lesson.
- Writing down key words in a notebook is helpful, though time-consuming.
- Highlighting English derivatives reinforces the key Latin words.
- The class can choose its favourite new English word each week. This word can then be displayed clearly somewhere in the classroom, along with its Latin root.
- The picture stories lend themselves to drama. Pupils invariably enjoy drama activities, which can vary from simply reading the story out loud in Latin in the classroom, to a much grander production for a school assembly. Pupils enjoy learning their lines and these words will never be forgotten.
- Some pupils will also be learning French or Spanish or may know another modern foreign language. Encourage them to make linguistic links.
- Encourage pupils to work in pairs on learning vocabulary; testing each other is relatively painless. Friends and older siblings can also help with the testing process.
- Some pupils like to learn words to a song or jingle.
- 'Little and often' is a good principle for vocabulary work, much better than presenting pupils with a daunting list of words.
- Classroom displays of vocabulary items, arranged thematically, can be very effective, for example words to do with the family, food or animals.
- There is a glossary of Latin words at the end of the Pupil's Book. Pupils will need to be taught how to use this. For example, explain that nouns are listed with their genders; adjectives are given in all three genders; verbs are listed in the first person present tense and infinitive forms.

Homework

Minimus is being taught in very different circumstances throughout the world, from English preparatory schools where pupils are expected to complete one or more Latin homeworks before the next class, to lunch-time or after-school voluntary clubs where half an hour disappears all too quickly and there is no formal reinforcement until the next lesson. It would therefore be inappropriate to be prescriptive about homework but here are a few suggestions.

- The photocopiable activity sheets in the Teacher's Resource Book provide valuable reinforcement activities. Even when they are presented as optional activities, many pupils enjoy completing them.

- Pupils enjoy competitions. Competitions involving art, creative writing, drama, Latin reading, etc. are fun for the pupils but also reinforce classwork.

Using the activity sheets

The photocopiable activity sheets have been designed to be flexible; there is no one correct way to use them. The way you use them will depend on the age and ability of your pupils. For example, with activity sheet IX (the map of Roman Britain) younger pupils will need help with locating and naming the Roman towns, whereas older pupils should be able to find most of them with the help of an atlas.

A short bibliography

Among the plethora of books on the Romans and Roman Britain, the following would be especially helpful when teaching *Minimus secundus*:

Women in Roman Britain Lindsay Allason-Jones, British Museum Publications, 1989 (ISBN 0 7141 1392 1)

Roman York Patrick Ottaway, Batsford/English Heritage, 1993 (ISBN 0 7134 7083 6)

Roman Clothing and Fashion Alexandra T. Croom, Tempus, 2002 (ISBN 0 7524 2512 9)

The Roman Soldier G.R. Watson, Thames & Hudson, 1985 (ISBN 0 500 27376 6)

As the Romans did Jo-Ann Shelton, Oxford University Press, 1998 (ISBN 0 195 08974 X)

A Companion to Roman Britain Peter Clayton (ed.), Phaidon, 1980 (ISBN 0 714 82031 8)

The Odyssey Homer (translated by E.V. Rieu, revised by Peter V. Jones), Penguin, 2003 (ISBN 0 140 44911 6)

The Ordnance Survey map of Roman Britain (ISBN 0 319 29029 8) would also be very useful for classroom display and for research purposes.

1 Iūlius
Last days at Vindolanda

- **subject matter:** the family prepares to leave Vindolanda
- **materials:** activity sheets I–IV
- **grammar content:** revision of grammar in *Minimus* – present tense verbs, subject and object

Picture story

A special occasion (pp. 6–7)

1 Lepidina and Iulius watch the parade.
Lepidina: The parade is approaching. The parade is magnificent!
Iulius: Yes!

2 Pandora calls Rufus.
Pandora: Rufus! Look at the horse!
Rufus: The horse is splendid. Hooray!

3 Rufus calls Corinthus.
Rufus: Look! Father is riding.
Corinthus: Yes. The horse is special!

4 Corinthus calls Candidus.
Corinthus: Candidus! Flavius is riding.
Candidus: The horse is magnificent!

5 The soldiers are approaching. Some are marching, others are riding.

6 *Soldiers:* Hooray! Flavius is the best commander.

7 Minimus and Vibrissa are sleeping.

8 Suddenly they hear the noise.
M&V: W-w-why is everyone excited?
Then Rufus explains the situation.

9 Minimus watches the parade. Vibrissa watches Minimus.
M&V: Hooray! We are happy!

10 *Everyone:* Goodbye! We thank you!

THE ART OF TRANSLATION

Pupils should be made aware that translation is a fine skill; there is rarely one perfect translation for any Latin word or phrase. Pupils should be encouraged to be bold and innovative, to listen to each other's suggestions and to choose the translation that seems to them to be the most appropriate in the context.

One important point to stress to pupils is that the present tense can be translated either by the simple or by the continuous present in English, so **appropinquat** may be translated either as 'he approaches' or as 'he is approaching'. Pupils must decide which sounds better on each occasion. These alternative translations of present tense verbs are given in the 'Words to help' section of chapter 1; thereafter, only the simple present is listed.

Grasp the grammar

1. he/she/it rides/is riding
2. they approach/are approaching
3. I call/am calling
4. we ride/are riding
5. he/she/it watches/is watching
6. I ride/am riding
7. you (pl.) approach/are approaching
8. you (pl.) watch/are watching
9. they ride/are riding
10. you (sing.) call/are calling
11. we watch/are watching
12. you (sing.) approach/are approaching

Latin roots

1. equestrian from **equus**, horse; **equitō**, I ride. Concerning horses.
2. vocal from **vocō**, I call; **vōx**, the voice. Concerning the voice.
3. spectators from **spectō**, I watch. People who watch.
4. military from **mīlitēs**, soldiers. Service as a soldier.
5. dormant from **dormiō**, I sleep. A sleeping volcano that may erupt at any time.
6. audio-visual from **audiō**, I hear and **videō**, I see. Things to listen to and look at.

Roman report

The photograph shows the horse's ceremonial head-dress (**chamfron**) from the museum at Vindolanda. Sufficient pieces of leather survived from the original for archaeologists to make this reconstruction.

Picture story

An important job (p. 10)

1 *Flavius:* Soldiers! Collect some logs!

2 The soldiers run into the forest. The soldiers cut some logs.

3 The soldiers build a bonfire.

4 Then the soldiers throw the writing tablets onto the bonfire.

Soldier 1: Why are we doing this?
Soldier 2: I don't know!

5 The slave girls carry hot lard and pour it onto the bonfire.

6 The soldiers rub flints. Suddenly the bonfire burns and the tablets burn.

7 Everyone is watching the flames.
Rufus approaches the bonfire.

8 *Pandora:* Rufus! Don't touch! Come here!
Rufus cries.

Grasp the grammar

Depending on the age and ability of the pupils, you may wish to use the terms **accusative** and **nominative case**. If pupils are not already familiar with these terms, you could introduce them as follows:

> There are special terms to describe the various jobs which nouns do in a Latin sentence: we call them 'cases'.
>
> The **nominative case** is the case of the **subject**. So in sentence **a**, we say that the bonfire (**rogus**) is in the nominative case.
>
> The **accusative case** is the case of the **object**. So in sentence **b**, the bonfire is in the accusative case and its ending changes accordingly (**rogum**).

1 Pandora (s) <u>calls</u> Rufus (o).
2 Lepidina (s) <u>watches</u> the procession (o).
3 Minimus (s) <u>hears</u> the noise (o).
4 Iulius (s) <u>explains</u> the situation (o).
5 Vibrissa (s) <u>watches</u> Minimus (o).
6 Everyone (s) <u>looks at</u> the flames (o).
7 The soldiers (s) <u>throw</u> the writing tablets (o).

Words to remember

Nouns
equus (m) horse
mīlitēs (m pl) soldiers
pompa (f) parade

Verbs
appropinquat he approaches/is approaching
audit he hears/is hearing
vocat he calls/is calling

Adjectives
laetus happy
optimus excellent/the best

Adverbs
subitō suddenly
tum then

Exclamations
ecce! look!
ēheu! oh no!
euge! hooray!

Idioms
aliī . . . aliī . . . some . . . others . . .
ita vērō yes

Greek myth

According to the legend, Bellerophon was crippled by his fall and wandered the earth.

Suggested activities

ART

- Draw Pegasus.
- Draw a picture of the bonfire, with the soldiers destroying the writing tablets.

DESIGN AND TECHNOLOGY

- Design a cardboard Chimaera with fire (red crêpe paper?) coming out of its mouth.

ENGLISH

- Write an acrostic poem about the Chimaera.
- Choose two characters (e.g. Lepidina and Rufus, Flavius and Rufus, Flavius and Minimus) and describe the parade from each one's point of view.
- Discuss the different types of evidence for life at Vindolanda (buildings, artefacts, writing tablets, inscriptions). Can you think of other things that are sometimes found on ancient sites, which help us to understand and to date them? (e.g. coins and pottery).

ARCHAEOLOGY

- Make a list of ten objects which you would choose to bury to reflect our society and which an archaeologist might dig up in 100 years' time (e.g. mobile phone, lap-top computer, pizza box, Barbie doll, cricket bat, coins). Compare notes and compile a class list of ten items. Make a large poster to illustrate these 'time capsule' items.
- Make a more personal list of ten objects that you would choose to bury to reflect your own particular interests and lifestyle. (Teachers can do this as well!) This should lead to lots of oral work as the class shares ideas.

PSHE

- Health and safety issues: discussion of fires. In the second picture story, women pour lard onto the fire to make it burn. Discuss what *not* to put on a fire and how to smother flames.

Activity sheet answers

ACTIVITY SHEET I

From left to right, the members of Flavius's household are: (back row) Corinthus, Candidus, Flavius, Lepidina, Iulius, Pandora, Flavia, Gaius; (front row) Rufus, Minimus, Vibrissa.

ACTIVITY SHEET III

Practice with the present tense

1 he/she/it nibbles/is nibbling
2 we moo/are mooing
3 you crawl/are crawling
4 he/she/it tramples/is trampling
5 they snore/are snoring
6 they nibble/are nibbling
7 you trample/are trampling
8 you stammer/are stammering
9 we stammer/are stammering
10 I crawl/am crawling
11 I moo/am mooing
12 you snore/are snoring

Practice with the verb 'to be'

1 sumus
2 est
3 sum
4 es
5 sunt
6 estis
7 Flāvius sum.
8 Pandōra es.
9 Minimus et Vibrissa sumus.
10 mīlitēs sunt.
11 Candidus et Corinthus estis.
12 Lepidīna est.

2 Augustus
Iulius joins the army

■ **subject matter:** the Roman army; the emperor Trajan ■ **materials:** activity sheets V–VIII
■ **grammar content:** gender; adjectives; adverbs

Picture story
A soldier at last! (pp. 13–14)

1 *Iulius:* Now I am a Roman soldier. I am very happy!
Rufus: Why are you so happy, Iulius?
Iulius: Because the Roman legions are very famous.

2 *Rufus:* Why are the Roman legions very famous?
Iulius: Because Roman soldiers are always winning.

3 *Iulius:* Now I am going to Dacia.
Rufus: Why are you going to Dacia?
Iulius: Because Trajan is fighting a war there.

4 *Rufus:* Who is Trajan?
Iulius: He is the Roman emperor, of course.
Flavius: Yes. Trajan is the best emperor.

5 *Rufus:* Where is Dacia?
Iulius: Dacia is across the sea. Dacia is near Germany.

6 Map.

7 *Rufus:* Oh no! It is a long journey. What are the soldiers doing there?

8 *Flavius:* The soldiers are building a bridge there.

9 *Rufus:* But war is dangerous. I am worried.
Iulius: War is also necessary.

10 *Flavius:* Don't be afraid, Rufus. The goddess Fortuna protects soldiers.

Grasp the grammar

Adjectives normally follow the noun they describe. However, adjectives which describe size or quantity usually precede the noun (e.g. **multī mīlitēs**). Even this rule is not hard and fast: Trajan soon acquired the title **optimus prīnceps** where the word **optimus** precedes its noun.
The concept of three genders may need further explanation. In particular, pupils need to realise that masculine and feminine words do not equate to male and female.

1 The legions are very famous.
legiōnēs (noun), **nōtissimae** (adjective)

2 Roman soldiers are always winning/always win.
mīlitēs (noun), **Rōmānī** (adjective)

3 Lepidina is not happy.
Lepidīna ([proper] noun), **laeta** (adjective)

4 War is dangerous.
bellum (noun), **perīculōsum** (adjective)

Latin roots

1 notable from **nōtus**, famous. He will be very famous.
2 principal from **prīnceps**, the leading citizen. The leading boy's part.
3 marina from **mare**, the sea. A place by the sea for mooring boats.
4 perilous from **perīculōsum**, dangerous.
5 timid from **timēre**, to be afraid. Frightened.
6 transatlantic from **trāns**, across. A flight across the Atlantic.

Background information: the emperor Trajan

Trajan's full name was Marcus Ulpius Traiana and he was emperor from AD 98 to 117. The following facts about Trajan's life are known from the accounts of Cassius Dio (historian), Suetonius (biographer) and Pliny, who wrote a long panegyric (public commendation) of Trajan in AD 100. Moreover, when Pliny was sent to help administer the province of Bithynia, he wrote to the emperor whenever he needed advice, which was frequently. Pliny records his letters and Trajan's replies in Book X of his letters.

Pupils may like to compile a biography of Trajan, using the following information:

1 Trajan's three names show that he was a Roman citizen, but he was born in Spain, near Seville.
2 He was the first non-Italian emperor.
3 When he assembled two new legions to fight the war in Dacia (Romania) they were named after him: 2nd Trajan and 30th Ulpian (**II Trāiāna** and **XXX Ulpiāna**).
4 He was born in AD 53.
5 He was adopted by the Emperor Nerva as his son and heir. This might lead to a comparison with the British royal family and the rules of hereditary succession.
6 Trajan was an unassuming and courteous man, respectful to the Roman senate.
7 He was a popular leader of soldiers. He mixed with them, ate with them and took a personal interest in them. He marched in front of his men and was a strict disciplinarian.
8 For relaxation, Trajan enjoyed hunting.
9 He was keen to extend the boundaries of the Roman Empire (cf. his successor, Hadrian, who concentrated on consolidating the territories that Rome already ruled). Under Trajan, the Roman Empire reached its greatest extent.
10 AD 101: invaded Dacia. 1st Dacian War.
11 AD 105: 2nd Dacian War.
12 He built a bridge over the Danube, a great achievement at this period.
13 In Rome, he celebrated his great victories over the Dacians with 123 days of games and 10,000 gladiators.
14 Dacia was a wealthy country. The spoils from Dacia financed an extensive building programme in Rome, including Trajan's Forum and Trajan's Column.
15 Trajan also supervised the building of a new harbour at Ostia, the port of Rome.
16 He provided for the poor, by giving **alimenta** (financial aid) to help defray the expense of children; he also intervened to help abused children.
17 He married Pompeia Plotina. They had no children.
18 He died in AD 117 in Asia Minor, after a stroke.
19 His title was **optimus prīnceps**; he was certainly one of the best Roman emperors.
20 In AD 100 Pliny delivered his panegyric; it would have taken about six hours to recite.

Trajan's Column

This famous landmark in Rome is another important source of evidence about the life of Trajan. It also tells us a great deal about the equipment and activities of Roman soldiers on campaign. It should be noted, however, that Trajan commissioned the building of the column to show himself in a good light. In chapter 5, Iulius writes home giving a different, slightly less heroic picture of the war in Dacia. Pupils should be encouraged to think about bias, prejudice and distortion in ancient sources. Comparisons could be made with modern journalism, and with the roles of, for example, royal correspondents and the Poet Laureate. These are sophisticated concepts but pupils should begin to consider the idea of reporting the same events from a number of different perspectives.

Note the following facts about the column:

1 It is 30 metres high (130 feet).
2 It is made from 20 blocks of marble.
3 The spiral frieze around it tells the story of the two Dacian wars.
4 There are 155 separate scenes on the frieze.
5 There are 2,500 figures on the frieze.
6 There are casts of the frieze in the Victoria and Albert Museum in London.

7 The theme is the majesty of Roman peace.

8 Battles account for only a quarter of the frieze.

9 There is only one wounded Roman soldier!

10 It took seven years to carve.

11 Originally, the column had a statue of Trajan at the top (cf. Nelson's column in Trafalgar Square).

12 This statue was replaced by one of Saint Peter in AD 1588.

13 The column was financed by the treasure from the Dacian Wars.

14 Trajan's ashes were buried at the foot of the column, in a golden urn.

15 It is possible to climb up inside the column.

Picture story

The family says goodbye (pp. 17–18)

1 Candidus cooks an excellent dinner. Everyone dines very well and drinks wine.

2 Pandora sings sweetly and dances skilfully.

3 Corinthus writes a little book.
Corinthus: Iulius, I have a present for you.

4 *Iulius:* Corinthus, I thank you! In this book there are many Greek stories.

5 Rufus and Iulius fight playfully. Then they laugh.

6 Lepidina gathers many clothes.
Lepidina: Iulius, take these clothes! Dacia is cold.

7 Flavius shows the weapons. Iulius looks at his weapons closely.

8 Iulius strokes Vibrissa. Vibrissa purrs gently.

9 Minimus squeaks and runs around Iulius.

10 *Everyone:* Goodbye, Iulius!
Lepidina: Goddess Fortuna! Look after my son!
Lepidina is crying.

Greek myth

A fuller account of Odysseus's encounter with the Sirens can be found in the 12th book of Homer's *Odyssey* (lines 39–55 and 165–200). We recommend the Penguin edition of *The Odyssey* (translated by E.V. Rieu and revised by Peter V. Jones, 2003, ISBN 0 140 44911 6).

Words to remember

Nouns
arma (n pl) weapons
bellum (n) war
cēna (f) dinner
dea (f) goddess
imperātor (m) emperor
legiōnēs (f pl) legions
mare (n) sea

Verbs
aedificō I build
habeō I have
superō I win

Question words
cūr? why?
quid? what?
quis? who?
ubi? where?

Conjunctions
quod because
sed but

Adverbs
nunc now
semper always

Suggested activities

ENGLISH

- Work in pairs: one of you is Trajan and one is Pliny. Invent a dialogue in which Pliny speaks with Trajan when he returns from Dacia. Perform the dialogue.
- Write a letter home from Iulius, describing the hazards of his journey to Dacia.
- Write Lepidina's diary, in which she expresses her fears for her son's safety, both on the journey and in Dacia.

ART

- Look at the paintings of Odysseus and the Sirens on the Minimus website (www.minimus-etc.co.uk). Study the paintings carefully and try to find the different parts of the story.

GEOGRAPHY

- Using an atlas, trace Iulius's probable route from Vindolanda to Romania. Discuss methods of transport.

  Then look at activity sheet V, the map of the Roman Empire. Mark in the route, naming all the countries that Iulius would pass through. Estimate how long the journey would have taken. Visit a travel agent or use the internet to find out how long it would take to fly from Newcastle to Romania today.

ICT

- Research Trajan on the internet.
- Give each pupil (or group of pupils) the name of a Roman emperor from the following list. Ask them to research the dates and some details of the emperor's reign. Then make a class timeline with the names and dates of all the Roman emperors. This can be displayed in the classroom.

31 BC–AD 14	Augustus
AD 14–37	Tiberius
AD 37–41	Caligula
AD 41–54	Claudius
AD 54–68	Nero
AD 68–69	Galba
AD 69	Otho
AD 69	Vitellius
AD 69–79	Vespasian
AD 79–81	Titus
AD 81–96	Domitian
AD 96–98	Nerva
AD 98–117	Trajan
AD 117–138	Hadrian
AD 138–161	Antoninus Pius
AD 161–180	Marcus Aurelius
AD 180–192	Commodus
AD 193	Pertinax
AD 193	Didius Julianus
AD 193–211	Septimius Severus

Activity sheet answers

ACTIVITY SHEET V

Iulius would travel by road to the river Humber. A small boat would take him to a larger ship in which he would cross the North Sea. Arriving in Germania Inferior, he would travel across Europe, eastwards to Dacia, avoiding the Alps. He would travel constantly through Roman provinces.

ACTIVITY SHEET VI

In the scene from Trajan's column, Dacians are seen swimming across the Danube to try to attack a Roman camp; Roman soldiers defend the camp.

ACTIVITY SHEET VII

Iulius's pack:

1	soap	✘
2	tin of sardines	✘
3	food pan	✓
4	grain	✓
5	socks	✓
6	spade	✓
7	wooden stakes	✓
8	mobile phone	✘
9	salt	✓
10	woollen hat	✓
11	letter	✓
12	water bottle	✓
13	photo	✘
14	dried fruit	✓
15	folding knife	✓
16	chocolate	✘

3 September
On the move

■ **subject matter:** travel; health ■ **materials:** activity sheets IX–XII
■ **grammar content:** infinitives and impersonal verbs

Picture story
A difficult journey (pp. 20–21)

1 The whole family is sitting in silence.
It is raining again.

2 The road is muddy.
The wagon moves forward slowly.

3 *Flavius:* Be careful! It is dangerous. The road is slippery.

4 Suddenly the wagon falls down into a ditch.

Lepidina: Oh no!

5 *Flavius:* You must/it is necessary for you to get down from the wagon.

The whole family gets down.

6 *Flavius:* It is difficult for me to push the wagon forward.
Candidus! Corinthus! Help!

7 At last the wagon is on the road.
The family climbs up onto the wagon again.

Lepidina: Hooray!

8 Now it is thundering. Rufus is terrified.
Pandora: I must sing.

9 It is becoming dark. At last they reach Cataractonium.

10 Flavia and her husband, called Gaius, welcome the family.

Flavia and Gaius: Come in! You are very welcome.

Grasp the grammar

1 It always rains in Britain.
2 Vibrissa says, 'It is raining again. It is necessary for me to run/I must run.'
3 Vibrissa says, 'It is difficult for me to run because I am fat.'
4 Lepidina says, 'Rufus, it is getting late/it is becoming dark. It is necessary for you to sleep/you must sleep.'
5 Rufus says, 'But it is difficult for me to sleep because I am not tired.'
6 Lepidina says, 'It is becoming dark. It is necessary for us to hurry/we must hurry.'
7 Flavius says, 'But it is difficult for us to hurry because the road is slippery.'
8 Rufus says, 'It is thundering again. I am terrified.'
9 Pandora says, 'Rufus, don't be afraid! I must sing.'
10 Rufus says, 'Now it is not thundering. Hooray!'

NB **necesse est** should be translated as 'it is necessary' at first, to reinforce the infinitive which follows it. Pupils should then be guided towards the more natural translations of 'must' or 'have to'.

The 13 impersonal verbs, in order, are: **pluit**, **pluit**, **necesse est**, **difficile est**, **advesperāscit**, **necesse est**, **difficile est**, **advesperāscit**, **necesse est**, **difficile est**, **tonat**, **necesse est** and **tonat**.

The eight infinitives are: **currere**, **currere**, **dormīre**, **dormīre**, **festīnāre**, **festīnāre**, **timēre** and **cantāre**.

Latin roots

1 lubricating from **lūbricus**, slippery. Oil to make the engine parts move smoothly.
2 propeller from **prōpellere**, to push forward.
3 cantata from **cantāre**, to sing. A sung version of a text.
4 sedentary from **sedēre**, to sit. A job that requires you to sit down.

lentē means 'slowly' in both Latin and Italian.

Background information: Cataractonium

In the first *Minimus* book, the eldest child, Flavia (named after her father), was 16. She is now 21 and married. As her family is important, she has married the commanding officer of the fort at the small town of Cataractonium (modern-day Catterick). Cataractonium is referred to several times in the Vindolanda writing tablets as a major stores base.

At this period, Cataractonium consisted mainly of a small settlement outside the fort, at the crossing of the River Swale. In the second century, a **mānsiō** or posting station was built. This had rooms for official travellers and its own suite of baths. There were also shops and a temple. Cataractonium grew in importance and there are some splendid artefacts from the settlement in the Yorkshire Museum in York. It is possible to see, for example, some fine wall-painting, a bronze statuette of Vulcan and a beautiful enamelled perfume flask. Although these artefacts date from a later period than that featured in this book, pupils can see that Cataractonium went on to become an important and prosperous town.

Picture story

Flavia is not well (pp. 24–25)

1. *Gaius:* Sit down, sir! You are very welcome.

2. Candidus inspects/looks at the dinner.

   Corinthus: The dinner is excellent, isn't it?
   Candidus: No. The dinner is ordinary. There is no peacock!

3. Flavius and Lepidina eat the excellent dinner. But Flavia eats nothing.

4. *Lepidina:* What's the matter, Flavia? Why are you not eating the food?
   Flavia: It is difficult for me to eat the food.

5. *Lepidina:* Why is it difficult?
   Flavia: Because I am being sick every day.

   Flavia goes out quickly.

6. Flavia returns to the dining room.

   Lepidina: You are pregnant!
   Flavia: Yes! I am pregnant.

7. *Flavius:* Hooray! Slaves! More wine! I must propose a toast. Congratulations!

8. Lepidina looks closely at Flavia.

   Lepidina: Where is a good midwife? You must rest.

9. *Flavius:* I will be a grandfather!
   Lepidina: I will be a grandmother!

   Lepidina and Flavius are happy.

10. But Lepidina is anxious.

   Lepidina: Mother goddesses! Look after my daughter!

(The mother goddesses were local Celtic goddesses. They are usually depicted in a group of three in Romano–British sculptures.)

Background information: pregnancy

An important writer on gynaecology in the Roman world was the 1st-century AD Greek doctor, Soranus, who came from Ephesus. He wrote about 20 books, including works on grammar and etymology. His work *On the Art of Surgery and Gynaecology* was among those translated into Latin, from Greek, in the Middle Ages. His theories will amuse pupils and will at times astonish them by their modernity, for example the recommended use of a birthing-chair and advice on breathing techniques during labour. What emerges is enormous respect for the experienced midwife. Male doctors tended to be called only for difficult births.

There is more information on Roman childbirth customs in chapter 7 when Flavia gives birth to twins – this would have come as a complete shock in pre-ultrasound days!

Words to remember

Noun
via (f) road

Adverbs
celeriter quickly
cotīdiē every day
iterum again
lentē slowly
tandem at last

Verbs
sedet she sits

Impersonal verbs
advesperāscit it is becoming dark
difficile est it is difficult
necesse est it is necessary/must
pluit it is raining
tonat it is thundering

Suggested activities

PSHE

- With older pupils it may be appropriate to discuss why pregnancy will carry greater risks for Flavia than for an expectant mother today. One might stress the quality of ante-natal care (pointing out the Latin root of 'ante-natal') and compare it with that of developing countries now, or even in fairly recent times in this country.

MATHS

- The journey from Vindolanda to York is about 193 km (120 miles). Catterick is about half-way.
  Practise working out the distances, in miles and kilometres, between Vindolanda and Catterick and then on to York. The family will travel about 6 km (4 miles) each hour. How long will the journey take? (On a map of Britain, pupils could find somewhere they know which is approximately 60 miles from their own town. This will help them to imagine the distance from Vindolanda to Catterick.)

  NB One of the Vindolanda tablets complains about the bad road to Cataractonium!

ENGLISH

- Pupils could write Flavia's diary during her pregnancy.
- Discuss why road travel was so hazardous in Roman times (cf. discussion of sea travel in chapter 2, when Iulius leaves for Dacia). Here are some issues to consider: lack of maps, no street lighting, few signposts, the danger of bandits, etc.

ART

- Make a long collage, with each pupil painting or drawing a different member of the family on the journey (i.e. Flavius on horseback; Lepidina, Rufus, the three slaves and two animals in the cart; the armed guard).

DRAMA

- Act out the story of the family's journey to Catterick.

LANGUAGES

- Following a class discussion, make a poster illustrating how to say 'it is raining' (and possibly other weather words) in several languages. Offer a prize for the best poster and create a class display.

GEOGRAPHY

- Use the Ordnance Survey map of Roman Britain. Find out which roads near you were originally Roman roads. Make a map of your area/county and mark in the Roman roads.

Activity sheet answers

ACTIVITY SHEET IX

1 **Vindolanda** – Chesterholm
2 **Luguvālium** – Carlisle
3 **Corstopitum** – Corbridge
4 **Pōns Aelius** – Newcastle upon Tyne
5 **Cataractōnium** – Catterick
6 **Eborācum** – York
7 **Dēva** – Chester
8 **Virocōnium** – Wroxeter
9 **Lindum** – Lincoln
10 **Ratae** – Leicester
11 **Glēvum** – Gloucester
12 **Corinium** – Cirencester
13 **Īsca Silurum** – Caerleon
14 **Aquae Sūlis** – Bath
15 **Īsca Dumnoriōrum** – Exeter
16 **Callēva** – Silchester
17 **Verulāmium** – St Albans
18 **Londinium** – London
19 **Camulodūnum** – Colchester
20 **Dubris** – Dover

ACTIVITY SHEET X

The verb families are:

1 **dormiō**/**dormīre**/to sleep/dormant
2 **spectō**/**spectāre**/to look at/spectator
3 **cantō**/**cantāre**/to sing/chant
4 **cōnsūmō**/**cōnsūmere**/to eat/consumer
5 **custōdiō**/**custōdīre**/to guard/custody
6 **currō**/**currere**/to run/current

ACTIVITY SHEET XII

1 **currus** (chariot)
2 **asinus** (donkey)
3 **equus** (horse)
4 **ambulō** (walk)
5 **lectīca** (litter)
6 **plaustrum** (wagon)

4 Octōber
A new way of life in Eboracum

■ **subject matter:** life in a Roman town, Eboracum ■ **materials:** activity sheets XIII–XVI
■ **grammar content:** pronouns

Picture story
Discovering Eboracum (pp. 27–28)

1 *Rufus:* Who's he?
Candidus: Look! Barates is here! He is my friend. Barates is a flag-seller.

2 —

3 *Rufus:* Who are you? Are you also a flag-seller?
Potter: No! I am a potter.

4 *Rufus:* What is it?
Potter: This is a pottery workshop. In the pottery there are bowls and jars.

5 *Rufus:* Who are you? Are you also a potter?
Blacksmith: No! I am a blacksmith.

6 *Rufus:* What is it?
Blacksmith: It is a forge. Look! There are nails and swords.

7 *Barates:* Across the river there is a warehouse. In the warehouse there is a lot of grain.

8 *Rufus:* It is a very big warehouse!
Barates: Yes. We must store grain.

9 There are many ships on the river. The family watches the ships.

10 *Barates:* Look! Ships with jars are arriving from France.

Grasp the grammar

Flavius and Lepidina arrive in Eboracum. **It** is much bigger than Vindolanda. **They** see Barates. **He** takes **them** to the river. **He** shows **them** the warehouse. **They** look at **it**. **They** say, '**It** is very big and **it** is near to the river.' Then **they** look at the ships. **They** are carrying goods from many different countries. Flavius says, 'Look at those jars on the ships.' Lepidina says, 'The jars are filled with wine from France and olive oil from Spain.'

Latin roots

The first five derivatives come from **multī**, many.

6 The gladiator was called Maximus from the Latin **maximus**, very big.

Roman report: Eboracum

The remains of Roman York span a period of about 350 years. Help pupils to understand its development from the early wooden military fortress housing the Ninth Legion and the settlement that grew up around it, to the prosperous and important town that was the base for the Sixth Legion. The area between the military fort and the river seems to have been rather crowded and noisy. It was probably fairly smelly too: the sewers which served the legion of 5,000 men emptied directly into the river, so disease was common. There was also a constant risk of fire in the wooden buildings.

The stories in this chapter are based on the archaeological finds around the region of the grain warehouse. Remains of beetles and charred grain, both clearly visible under the microscope, are an unusual source of evidence about Roman life.

Picture story
The granary is destroyed (pp. 31–32)

1 *Rufus:* Father! Mother! Look! The workmen are destroying the granary.

2 The family watches the workmen. The workmen are removing the planks.

3 *Workmen:* Hooray! It is easy for us to destroy the granary.

4 *Foreman:* Workmen! Stop! You must remove the planks carefully. Wood is expensive.

5 *Flavius:* Look, Rufus! Now the workmen are working carefully.

Rufus: But why are the workmen destroying the granary?

6 *Foreman:* Because the grain is bad.

7 *Lepidina:* Why is the grain bad?

Foreman: Because there are many beetles in the grain. We must destroy the granary.

8 *Rufus:* Where are the beetles?

Foreman: Look! There are thousands of beetles in the grain.

9 *Lepidina:* Rufus! Beetles are disgusting. Don't touch!

10 *Rufus:* No! Beetles are lovely.

Lepidina: Rufus! You must wash your fingers! Come with me!

Words to remember

Nouns	Verbs
amīcus (m) friend	**facile est** it is easy
amphorae (f pl) jars	**labōrāre** to work
flūmen (n) river	
frūmentum (n) grain	**Adjectives**
nāvēs (f pl) ships	**malus/a/um** bad
	maximus/a/um very big

Suggested activities

ART

- Imagine and draw a picture of the Hydra.
- Use activity sheet XIV to make your own Hydra!

ICT

- Research the Twelve Labours of Heracles (Hercules) on the internet. Then design a series of 12 posters on computer, each poster illustrating one of Heracles's tasks.

ENGLISH

- Work in pairs or small groups. Tell the rest of the class about one of the twelve labours.
- In the school library and at home, find mythology books that tell the story of Heracles. You could use activity sheet XIII to illustrate the twelve labours. This could be a class competition with a small prize for the best entry.
- Find pictures of the twelve labours on Greek vases. (Teacher could make copies of such pictures for pupils to identify.)

CITIZENSHIP

- The family has moved from the countryside into Eboracum. Although Eboracum is still in the early stages of its development, they will experience the pleasures and dangers of living in a comparatively large town. Discuss the comparative benefits of town and country life.

POETRY

- Read Horace's tale of the town mouse and the country mouse (*Satires* II: 6 79–117). Which way of life do pupils prefer and why?

PRACTICAL ARCHAEOLOGY

- Use activity sheets XV and XVI to carry out an experiment in practical archaeology.

5 November
News from near and far

■ **subject matter:** life in the Roman army ■ **materials:** activity sheets XVII–XXI
■ **grammar content:** more impersonal verbs

Picture story

Sad news (pp. 34–35)

1 *Lepidina:* Dearest, why are you so sad?
Flavius: Because Duccius is dead.

2 *Lepidina:* Who is Duccius?
Flavius: Lucius Duccius Rufinus was an excellent soldier. He was a standard-bearer.

3 *Rufus:* What is a standard-bearer?
Flavius: A standard-bearer carries the standard into battle.

4 *Flavius:* The standard-bearer also looks after the pay. The standard-bearer keeps the pay safe underneath the shrine.

5 *Flavius:* I want to find an excellent sculptor.
Flavius goes out quickly.

6 Flavius enters the workshop.
Flavius: Hello!
Sculptor: Hello! What do you want?

7 *Flavius:* A standard-bearer called Lucius Duccius Rufinus is dead. I want you to make a splendid inscription.
Sculptor: Yes. It is easy for me to carve an inscription.

8 —

9 After a few days Flavius and Lepidina and Rufus return to the sculptor.
Rufus: I want to watch the sculptor.
Lepidina: You are allowed to watch the sculptor.

10 *Rufus:* Look at the standard! Look at the medals!
Lepidina: Oh dear! Duccius was a young man.

Note From this point, nouns are listed in Words to help in the nominative rather than in the form in which they appear in the text. Adjectives are given in the masculine, feminine and neuter nominative forms.

Grasp the grammar

The five infinitives, in order, are: **invenīre** (to find), **facere** (to make), **sculpere** (to carve), **spectāre** (to watch), **spectāre** (to watch).

Latin roots

1 custody from **custōdīre**, to keep safe.
2 voluntary from **volō**, I want. Sixth-formers can choose whether they want to do these games.
3 licensed from **tibi licet**, you are allowed. Allowed to kill.
4 juvenile from **iuvenis**, a young man. Behaving like a young person or child.
5 post-mortem and mortuary from **mortuus**, dead, **mors**, death and **post**, after. Examination of a body to discover the cause of death. A place where bodies are stored.
6 invention from **invenīre**, to discover/find.

Roman report: military standards

At the beginning of the second century AD, the Roman standard consisted of a long pole to which were attached several metal discs called **phalerae**. These discs were medals and commemorated previous victories won by that unit of soldiers. Above the discs there was sometimes a metal plaque, on which the name of the section (**cohort**) of the army was written. Above that, there might be a hand, often surrounded by a wreath. The standard was rather like a lucky mascot. It was carried into battle and it was a sign of encouragement for the soldiers.

THE TOMBSTONE

This tombstone, originally brightly coloured, is in the Yorkshire Museum and has been dated to the late first or early second century AD. It was found in 1688 in the churchyard wall of Holy Trinity Church, making it one of the first discoveries of Roman York. It stood in a niche beside the great Roman road, which approached York from the south-west.

Lucius Duccius Rufinus is one of only two men of the Ninth Legion from York whose name we know. The Ninth Legion is shown in the inscription; the Roman numerals may need some clarification, since they are written in the earlier form (VIIII and not IX). Lucius Duccius died at the age of 28. He came from Vienne in Gaul, in the Rhône valley, and he is shown wearing a twisted necklace, called a **torc**. It is hard to see whether he is wearing greaves and/or boots. The writing tablets may represent his will. Certainly he could read and write. His tombstone illustrates that young men who joined the Roman army at this time came from various locations: men from Gaul entered the Roman army in large numbers.

Although there is no known historical connection between Lucius Duccius and Flavius, the story envisages that Flavius mourns Lucius because he knew him well. Flavius takes care of his funeral and tombstone because Lucius is far from home with no family. No one knows the cause of Lucius Rufinus's death.

HSE at the foot of the tombstone stands for **hīc situs est** (here he lies). There is no mention of any heir. Sometimes, if the tombstone was commissioned by the heir, he would be named in the inscription, with the formula HFC, **hērēs faciendum cūrāvit** (his heir organised the making of it).

Picture story

A letter from Dacia (pp. 38–39)

1. Lepidina is happy. Lepidina is holding a letter. Lepidina reads the letter.
2. *Iulius writes:*
   Dacia is cold. It is often raining.
3. Now it is snowing!
4. Some soldiers are building a bridge.
5. The bridge goes across the Danube. The bridge is wonderful. There are many stones.
6. The soldiers have to work hard and carry the stones.
7. Other soldiers are fighting bravely. However, I am not fighting because I am a secretary/clerk.
8. Trajan is an excellent leader. Trajan eats with his soldiers.
9. *Everyone:* Hooray! Iulius is safe!
   Flavius and Rufus and the slaves are happy.
10. But Lepidina is anxious, because she is a mother.
    Lepidina: Dacia is cold. War is dangerous . . .

Background information: the bridge over the Danube

This account of Trajan's achievement comes from the historian Cassius Dio:

'Trajan constructed over the Danube a stone bridge for which I cannot sufficiently admire him. Brilliant, indeed, as are his other achievements, this surpasses them. For it has twenty piers of squared stone 150 feet in height above the foundations and 60 in width, and these, standing at a distance of 170 feet from one another, are connected by arches. How, then, could one fail to be astonished at the expenditure made upon them, or at the way in which each of them was placed in a river so deep, in water so full of eddies, and on a bottom so muddy?' (*Roman History*, LXVIII vi I)

Trajan's bridge over the Danube was the longest permanent bridge in the ancient world. Hadrian later dismantled it to prevent easy access to the empire by hostile intruders but the piles were left in place to show that there was nothing which could not be achieved by human ingenuity. The bridge was designed by Apollodorus of Damascus, who was also responsible for Trajan's column. Pupils may be amused to know that nowadays the national car in Romania is called a Dacia!

Words to remember

Noun
iuvenis (m) young man

Verbs
erat he was
intrat he enters
reveniunt they return

Infinitives
facere to make/to do
invenīre to find

Adverb
tamen however

Suggested activities

ENGLISH

- Write an imaginary biography of Lucius Duccius Rufinus, from when he joined the Roman army in Vienne up to his period of office in Eboracum. Include as many of the facts we have about him as you can.
- How many English words can you make from the letters found in the word **Romania**?
- Imagine you are Iulius. Write another letter home from Dacia.
- Taking the myth of Demeter and Persephone as your starting point, make up your own myth about a natural phenomenon such as snow or thunder.
- Three pupils describe the war in Dacia. One takes the part of Pliny, one of Trajan and one of Iulius. Compare events from these three different perspectives.

ART/DESIGN

- Design your own personal standard. Instead of **phalerae**, draw some discs and include your own medals for things that you are good at.
- Visit the Victoria and Albert Museum in London to see the casts of Trajan's column. Sketch your favourite scene.

GEOGRAPHY

- Use an atlas to trace Lucius Duccius's journey from Vienne to Eboracum.

PSHE

- Discuss the pros and cons of a compulsory period of military service.

Activity sheet answers

ACTIVITY SHEET XVIII

1. Flavius is from the Netherlands.
2. Corinthus is from Greece.
3. Duccius is from Vienne in Gaul.
4. Candidus and Pandora are from northern Britain.
5. Barates is from Palmyra in Syria.
6. Trajan is from Seville in Spain.

ACTIVITY SHEET XX

1. Duccius has to look after the pay.
2. It is easy for Duccius to carry the standard.
3. It is difficult for Duccius to fight.
4. Duccius likes to polish the decorations/medals.
5. Duccius is allowed to lead the soldiers.

ACTIVITY SHEET XXI

hodiē today
ningit it is snowing
pluit it is raining
sōl lūcet the sun is shining
tonat there is thunder
ventōsum est it is windy
nūbēs adsunt it is cloudy

6 December
Time for celebration!

■ **subject matter:** the Saturnalia festival ■ **materials:** activity sheets XXII–XXIV
■ **grammar content:** subject and object; impersonal verbs with infinitives

Picture story
It's the Saturnalia! (pp. 41–42)

1 The Saturnalia is here. Flavia and Gaius are visiting.

2 Lepidina cooks dinner.

3 Candidus tastes the food.

Candidus: The food is excellent!

4 Pandora reclines on a couch. Pandora is wearing a cap (of freedom).

5 Corinthus and Candidus are also reclining. Corinthus and Candidus are wearing caps.

6 Flavius and Rufus are carrying the food.

Flavius & Rufus: Today we are slaves!

7 Rufus is pouring the wine quickly.

Rufus: It is easy for me to pour the wine!

8 Rufus spills the wine! Rufus is crying.

Rufus: Oh no!

9 *Pandora:* Don't cry!

Flavius cleans up the wine.

10 *Corinthus:* How kind she is!
Candidus: And how beautiful!

Grasp the grammar

Remind pupils of the alternative translations of the present tense (he cries/he is crying).

1 he/she/it cries
2 they visit
3 he/she/it reclines
4 they recline
5 they carry
6 they cry
7 he/she/it visits
8 he/she/it pours
9 he/she/it carries

There is also a reminder of case endings here. As before, use the terms **nominative** and **accusative** case if you feel it to be appropriate for your pupils, for example:

The **nominative case** is the case of the **subject**. So in sentence **a**, we say that **Pandōra** is in the nominative case.

The **accusative case** is the case of the **object**. So in sentence **b**, **Pandōram** is in the accusative case.

Roman report: Saturnalia

There are many parallels between Christmas celebrations and Roman customs: most important festival, a long holiday, feasting, excitement, shows, jokes, party hats and hats in crackers (cf. **pilleus**), presents, candles. You may wish to make parallels with other religious festivals as appropriate.

Picture story
Time for presents! (pp. 44–45)

1 After dinner, Lepidina dances skilfully.

2 All the slaves sing merrily.

3 The whole family is telling/making jokes.

4 *Lepidina:* I must find the presents.

Lepidina goes out.

5 Lepidina returns to the dining room.

Lepidina: Rufus! This is your present!

Rufus receives a ball.

6 *Lepidina:* Corinthus! This is your present!

Corinthus receives a book.

7 *Lepidina:* Candidus! This is your present!

Candidus receives a candle.

8 *Lepidina:* My dearest! This is your present!

Flavius receives a ring.

9 *Flavius:* Lepidina! This is your present!

Lepidina also receives a ring.

10 *Minimus & Vibrissa:* Where are our presents?
Lepidina: Look!

Grasp the grammar

a difficile est mihi dōna invenīre.

b facile est mihi dōna invenīre.

Latin roots

1 benign from **benignus**, kind. The growth is not dangerous.

2 donation from **dōnum** (plural **dōna**), a present.

3 detergent from **dētergere**, to wipe clean. A cleaning solution.

4 post-natal from **post**, after and **nātus**, born. A clinic for small babies.

Background information: Saturnalia presents

Muddled presents

There is more than one correct solution to this puzzle. Here are suggestions for appropriate presents:

Flavius: **vēnābula**, hunting spears. See chapter 9 for an account of hunting as entertainment. Several of the Vindolanda tablets describe hunting expeditions, hunting dogs, etc.

Gaius: **ūdōnēs**, socks.

Flavia: **capillāmentum**, wig. Hair extensions were fashionable at this period.

Rufus: **pila**, ball.

Pandora: **sāpō**, hair dye. Blonde hair was very fashionable and colouring the hair was common.

Candidus: **scōpae**, broom.

Corinthus: **scrīnium**, bookcase. An appropriate gift for the educated slave.

Lepidina: **ampulla**, perfume flask.

Possible presents for Minimus and Vibrissa: **cāseus** (cheese), **pila** (ball), **mūs** (toy mouse), **piscis** (a fish).

Roman intaglios

The rings that Flavius and Lepidina exchange as Saturnalia presents are set with fine carved gemstones or *intaglios*. These particular intaglios were found in the sewer at Eboracum. Almost certainly, the stones became loose over a period of time and fell out in the baths.

The delicate carving of ancient stones and glass, without the help of magnification, is quite astonishing. Intaglios were often carved from semi-precious stones, especially jasper and carnelian. It is thought that young boys – perhaps as young as Rufus – carried out this delicate work while their eyesight was still good. They would have been apprenticed, possibly to their father or to another relative, and would have watched him at work. The largest and finest collection of these stones in Britain was found at the Roman fortress of Caerleon, in South Wales. The intaglios were found in the main drain in the bath-house and the collection is imaginatively displayed in the Caerleon museum. This excellent museum is well worth a visit.

Flavius's ring has an intaglio of Mars, the god of war, an appropriate god for a soldier.

Lepidina's shows Fortuna, the goddess of luck. Fortuna is an appropriate goddess for Lepidina, since she is the goddess often worshipped by soldiers. Lepidina prayed to her when Iulius left for Dacia in chapter 2.

Martial's descriptions of Saturnalia presents

There is evidence that Saturnalia celebrations were popular in Roman Britain. In letters between two slaves at Vindolanda, they discuss the cost of gifts for the Saturnalia. The Roman poet Martial (*c.* AD 40–104), usually known for his satirical tone, devotes the fourteenth book of the epigrams to descriptions of Saturnalia gifts. Pupils may enjoy some of these: some of the Latin words have a very pleasing sound. The following list will be useful if you choose to act this story out.

ampulla pōtiōna	drinking flask
auriscalpium	earpick
calathī	goblets
cithara	lyre
concha	seashell
crepitāculum	small rattle
crīnēs	hair
dentiscalpium	toothpick
pectinēs	combs
pīca	magpie
psittacus	parrot
pugiō	dagger
soleae lānātae	wool-lined slippers
spongea	sponge
strigilēs	scrapers (for the baths)
tabula lūsōria	gaming-board
tālī eboreī	ivory knucklebones*
tesserae	dice
tintinnābulum	bell
umbella	sunshade

* Knucklebones were used by Roman children to play an equivalent of the playground game 'jacks'.

NB Activity sheet XXIV features some of Martial's Saturnalia poems.

Greek myth

SATURN AND THE GOLDEN AGE

Several passages of Virgil refer to the period when Saturn ruled over Latium (an area south of Rome). Here is one of Virgil's descriptions of this Golden Age:

> 'These woods used to be the haunt of native fauns and nymphs and a race of men born from the hard wood of oak tree trunks. They had no rules of conduct and no civilisation. They did not know how to yoke oxen for ploughing, how to gather wealth or husband what they had, but they lived off the fruit of the tree and the harsh diet of huntsmen. In those early days, in flight from the weapons of Jupiter, came Saturn from heavenly Olympus, an exile who had lost his kingdom. He brought together this wild and scattered mountain people, gave them laws and resolved that the name of the land should be changed to Latium, since he had lain hidden within its borders. His reign was what men call the Golden Age, such was the peace and serenity of the people under his rule. But gradually a worse age of baser metal took its place and with it came the madness of war and the lust for possessions.'
>
> (*Aeneid*, VIII, 314–327)

(For other Virgil passages on the Golden Age, see *Aeneid*, VI, 792–4, *Aeneid*, VII, 48–9, *Georgics*, II, 536–40.)

However, the satirical writer Juvenal (early 2nd century AD) describes the reign of Saturn in a very different way:

> 'Chastity lingered on earth, they say, in the reign of Saturn.
> She was long to be seen in the days when a freezing cave provided a tiny home, complete with hearth and household gods,
> And enclosed both herds and owners within a communal gloom,
> In the days when a mountain wife would spread her woodland couch
> With leaves and straw and skins of beasts who lived in the district.
> Giving her breasts, with plenty to drink, to her mighty babes,
> She was often more uncouth than her acorn-belching husband.'
>
> (*Satires*, VI, 1–11)

Words to remember

Nouns
cibus (m) food
dōnum (n) present
lectus (m) couch
liber (m) book

Adverb
hodiē today

Adjective
pulcher/pulchra/pulchrum beautiful

Verbs
facit it makes
fundit he pours
lacrimat he cries
revenit she returns

Suggested activities

DRAMA

- Both the picture stories in this chapter lend themselves to drama. If performed in English, pupils could add to the dialogue by exploring the feelings of all the characters in their new roles, for example the slaves enjoying their freedom and being waited on.

ENGLISH

- Write the diary of Pandora, Corinthus or Candidus as he/she prepares to celebrate the Saturnalia and then during the festival itself.
- Discuss and then compare the two views of the Golden Age of Saturn given above. Compare Juvenal's satirical tone with that of modern satirical writers or TV programmes.
- Starting with *post-natal*, list as many derivatives as you can that involve **post**, for example *postpone*, *post-mortem*, *postscript*. Use a dictionary to add to the list. (You could draw a *postbox* and write all the words inside.)

ART

- Visit the National Gallery to look at paintings based on Classical myths.

Activity sheet answers

ACTIVITY SHEET XXII

1 **ante meridiem** before midday
2 **post meridiem** after midday
3 **et cetera** and the rest
4 **id est** that is
5 **quid prō quō** what for what (what in exchange for what)
6 **exemplī grātiā** for the sake of an example
7 **ad nauseam** to the point of being sick
8 **ad hoc** for this moment
9 **sine quā nōn** without which not (cannot exist without this)
10 **post scrīptum** an addition to what has been written
11 **per sē** in itself
12 **annō Dominī** in the year of the Lord
13 **nōtā bene** note well
14 **prō tempore** for the moment
15 **ad libitum** for pleasure

ACTIVITY SHEET XXIII

1 Candidus (s) tastes (v) the food (o).
2 Flavius (s) and Rufus (s) are carrying (v) the food (o).
3 Corinthus (s) is wearing (v) a cap (o).
4 Minimus (s) and Vibrissa (s) are eating (v) the food (o).
5 Rufus (s) is eating (v) the food (o).
6 Pandora (s) loves (v) Rufus (o).

7 Iānuārius
New beginnings

■ **subject matter:** birth ■ **materials:** activity sheets XXV–XXVIII
■ **grammar content:** imperatives

Picture story
The great day arrives (pp. 48–49)

1 Lepidina returns to Cataractonium.

Lepidina: I must help Flavia.

2 *Flavia:* The baby is arriving now! Help! Mother, help!

Flavia is in very great pain.

3 *Lepidina:* Don't be afraid! I must call for the midwife.
Flavia: Yes. Quickly!

4 The midwife arrives.

Midwife: Don't be afraid. Flavia, you are strong. Lepidina, bring water!

5 Lepidina brings water and towels. Then the midwife and Lepidina wash their hands (*lit.* fingers).

6 The midwife is helping Flavia.

Midwife: Flavia! Don't be worried! Relax!

7 Meanwhile Gaius is worried. Gaius is walking up and down/here and there.

8 *Midwife:* Look! Now the baby is here. Hooray! It is a little daughter!

9 *Midwife:* But wait! Another baby is here! Now it is/there is a son!

10 *Lepidina:* Flavia and the twins are safe!
Midwife: And you are a grandmother! Congratulations!

Grasp the grammar

Orders: **adiuvā**! (help!) **portā**! (carry!/bring!) **relaxā**! (relax!) **manē**! (wait!).

Negative orders: **nōlī** is the singular form of 'don't'; **nōlīte** is the plural.

1 Wash your fingers (or hands)! *plural*
2 Don't sleep! *plural*
3 Don't cry! *singular*
4 Carry/bring water! *plural*
5 Don't run! *singular*
6 Hurry! *plural*
7 Sing! *plural*
8 Don't fight! *plural*
9 Build! *singular*
10 Come in! *plural*

Latin roots

1 aqueduct from **aqua**, water and **dūcere**, to lead. A structure, often a bridge, to carry water across a valley.
2 maximum from **maximī**, a very large number. The greatest possible number.
3 valid from **validus**, strong. Not a good/acceptable excuse.
4 invalid from **validus**, strong. A sick/weak person.
5 obstetrics from **obstetrīx**, a midwife. The branch of medicine concerned with childbirth.

Picture story
Everyone welcomes the twins (pp. 51–52)

1 Gaius enters the bedroom. Gaius puts the twins onto the ground.

2 Suddenly the twins wail. Everyone is happy.

Gaius: The twins are strong. The household gods accept/receive/welcome the twins.

3 The midwife washes the twins and wraps them up.

4 Gaius holds the twins.

Gaius: How beautiful they are!

5 Flavius and Rufus come in.

Lepidina: You are a grandfather!
Flavius: And you are a grandmother!
Rufus: And I am an uncle!

6 *Gaius:* We must send for/summon an astrologer.

Gaius goes out.

7 The astrologer examines the stars and enters.

8 *Astrologer:* The twins have been born under the sign of the goat. The horoscope is good!

9 The astrologer holds the son.

Astrologer: This boy will be brave and strong.

10 The astrologer holds the daughter.

Astrologer: This girl will be strong and virtuous.

Roman report: having a baby

Perhaps inevitably, much of ancient birthing practice was haphazard. The crucial figure was the midwife, who was held in great respect, although standards of hygiene were variable. Soranus recommends that a good midwife should have 'short finger-nails, long fingers and should show strength of mind and body'. As well as the midwife, it seems that a number of female relatives might also be present when a woman gave birth. After lying on a bed for a while, the pregnant woman was often transferred to a birthing stool. A sculpture from Ostia shows a midwife helping a woman to give birth in this way; the midwife's assistant stands behind the mother to restrain her! The sound of bells was thought to ease the pain of women in childbirth.

The moment after birth, the father assumed an important role. First he placed the baby on the hearth to be accepted by the household gods. Then, if the baby appeared to be worth rearing, he would lift it up: this was called **susceptiō** (adoption).

The Romans tended to use wet-nurses, though Tacitus praises German women for breast-feeding their own babies. Soranus urges that 'a wet-nurse should know Greek, so that the infant may become accustomed to the best speech'.

Greek myth

- **Storytelling:** in another version of the myth, Remus taunts his brother by jumping over his city walls and mocking them. Take this opportunity to talk to pupils about the way that myths change in retelling. You could make comparisons with 'Chinese whispers', or ask pupils to tell their own versions of a recent national event and then compare newspaper articles about the same event. Pupils should begin to appreciate the way in which the individual interests and bias of each storyteller will alter the narrative. This could lead in to a much bigger project on oral storytelling. You could focus on the oral epic technique of Homer in the *Iliad* and the *Odyssey*.
- **Visual images:** the she-wolf suckling the twins became a common image of Ancient Rome and it appeared on coins. There is a famous bronze statue depicting it in the Capitoline Museum in Rome. The twins themselves are not Roman originals but are a Renaissance addition. The mosaic in the Pupil's Book is another depiction of the scene.

Words to remember

Nouns
cubiculum (n) bedroom
fīlia (f) daughter
fīlius (m) son
terra (f) earth, land, ground

Adjective
fortis/fortis/forte brave

Preposition
sub under

Verbs (now given in the ***infinitive*** form)
accipere to receive
adiuvāre to help
advenīre to arrive
pōnere to put
revenīre to return

Suggested activities

ICT

- Research the twelve signs of the Zodiac.
- Research the word 'January'; find out about Janus. Report back to the class.
- Research all twelve months of the year and find out why they are so called.

ART

- Make a poster showing the twelve signs of the Zodiac; include the Latin name for each sign. They are as follows:

Aquarius	water-carrier
Pisces	fish
Aries	ram
Taurus	bull
Gemini	twins
Cancer	crab
Leo	lion
Virgo	girl
Libra	scales
Scorpio	scorpion
Sagittarius	centaur
Capricorn	goat

See also activity sheet XXV.

ENGLISH

- Collect a list of onomatopoeic words in English and/or Latin. Illustrate them on a poster.
- In what ways do people try to see into the future now? Pupils can use activity sheet XXVIII to research Roman methods of predicting the future and compare them with modern approaches. Remind pupils that **ōmen** is a Latin word. Then discuss whether or not it is a good idea to seek to know the future.

PSHE

- Broaden the discussion on omens to include superstition. The Romans were highly superstitious. For example, the left was regarded as unlucky (the Latin for left is **sinister**) so Romans liked to enter a room right foot first. (Compare this with our superstition about not walking under ladders.) Certain days were regarded as lucky and others as unlucky in the Roman calendar.
- A major undertaking such as a sea voyage required prayers and sacrifices to the appropriate deity (usually Neptune). This could lead to a discussion on the differences between religion, superstition and tradition.

Activity sheet answers

ACTIVITY SHEET XXVI

Family members labelled as follows:

Lepidina	
avia	grandmother
māter	mother
Flavius	
avus	grandfather
pater	father
Rufus	
fīlius	son
avunculus	uncle
frāter	brother
Baby girl	
fīlia	daughter
īnfāns	baby
gemina	female twin
soror	sister
neptis	grand-daughter
Baby boy	
frāter	brother
īnfāns	baby
geminus	male twin
nepōs	grandson

ACTIVITY SHEET XXVII

1	**nōlī strīdēre!**	Don't squeak!
2	**sedē!**	Sit down!
3	**nōlīte pugnāre!**	Don't fight!
4	**nōlī dormīre!**	Don't sleep!
5	**intrā!**	Come in!
6	**nōlī lacrimāre!**	Don't cry!
7	**exite!**	Go out!
8	**cavēte!**	Watch out!
9	**cāseum cōnsūme!**	Eat the cheese!

ACTIVITY SHEET XXVIII

An **astrologer** studied the stars.

A **haruspex** was a special type of priest who sacrificed animals and then inspected their internal organs, especially the liver, to predict the future.

An **augur** was another kind of priest who examined the flight of birds as a means of foretelling the future.

An **oracle** interpreted messages from the gods. (See chapter 8 for information about the most famous oracle at Delphi.)

8 Februārius
Time for some Greek

- **subject matter:** Roman seafaring; the oracle at Delphi
- **materials:** activity sheets XXIX–XXXII
- **grammar content:** imperfect tense

Picture story
Rufus's first Greek lesson (pp. 55–56)

NB Corinthus is now too busy to teach Rufus Greek. He is secretary to Flavius in his new civilian post as he supervises the construction of the new military headquarters.

1 Demetrius enters.
Flavius: Hello, teacher! This is Rufus.

2 *Flavius:* Rufus! Demetrius is the new teacher.
Rufus: Hello!
Demetrius: Hello, Rufus!

3 *Rufus:* Where are you living?/Where do you live?
Demetrius: Now I live in Eboracum but recently I was sailing around Scotland.

4 *Rufus:* And weren't you frightened?
Demetrius: Yes. A storm was blowing.

5 *Demetrius:* It was windy and raining heavily. The sea was stormy.

6 *Demetrius:* The storm was tossing the ship on the sea. The sailors and I were terrified.

7 *Demetrius:* Every day I was praying because I was afraid. At last we were sailing into the harbour.

8 *Sailors:* We are safe! We must thank the gods.

9 *Demetrius:* I wanted to donate tablets. These are the tablets.

10 *Rufus:* But it is difficult to read the tablets!
Demetrius: Yes! The letters are Greek/They are Greek letters.

Grasp the grammar

Examples of the imperfect tense:

Pic. 3	**nāvigābam**	I was sailing
Pic. 4	**timēbās**	you were afraid/frightened
	efflābat	it was blowing
Pic. 5	**pluēbat**	it was raining
Pic. 6	**iactābat**	it was tossing
	timēbāmus	we were afraid
Pic. 7	**ōrābam**	I was praying
	timēbam	I was frightened
	nāvigābāmus	we were sailing
Pic. 9	**volēbam**	I was wanting

Latin roots

1 navigation from **nāvigāre**, to sail.
2 mariner from **mare**, the sea. A sailor.
3 naval from **nāvis**, a ship.
4 habitat from **habitāre**, to live.
5 turbulence from **turbulentus**, stormy.
6 tempest from **tempestās**, a storm. The first scene of *The Tempest* is a terrible storm at sea.

Background information: Scribonius Demetrius

Scribonius Demetrius was a **grammaticus** who would normally have taught older boys. Nevertheless, in this well-to-do family it would be quite normal for even a young boy like Rufus to be taught Greek, such was the increasing Romanisation of Britain which Tacitus refers to in the *Agricola*.

This Demetrius may be the same Demetrius of Tarsus who met Plutarch at Delphi in AD 83 on a visit to consult the oracle. It is thought that he spent some years in York, probably on the staff of Fronto, commander of the Ninth Legion from AD 76 to 79. Demetrius was the author of the two bronze votive tablets, which are now in the Yorkshire Museum. These two tablets, written in Greek in punched dots, are thanks offerings for a safe voyage around the Western Isles of Scotland. The two tablets were found in 1840, near the old railway station on the far side of the River Ouse, opposite the site of the fortress. They were made of bronze (originally silvered) and were intended to be nailed up in a shrine in the bath-house.

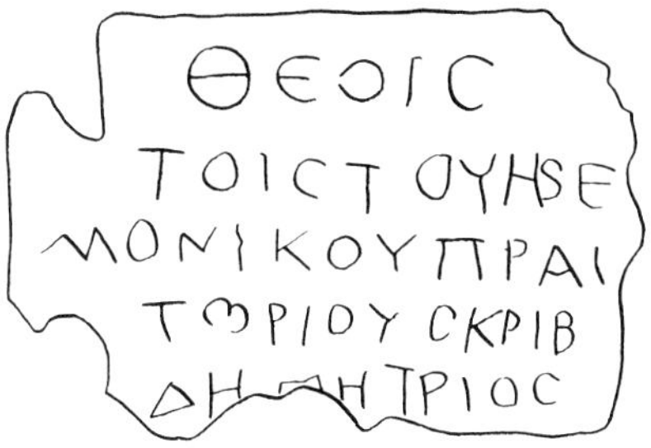

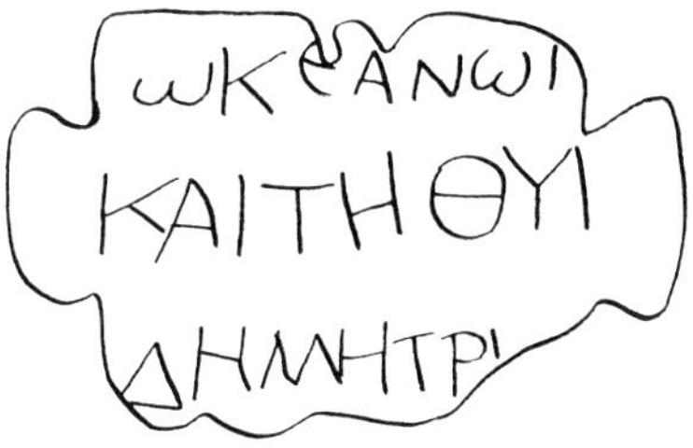

Demetrius was very relieved to have returned safely from his sea voyage. The dangers of sailing in the ancient world are well attested. A useful parallel might be drawn with Roman Alexandria, where a special parade was held on 5 March each year, to celebrate the beginning of spring and the start of the sailing season.

Picture story

Rufus learns his letters (pp. 59–60)

1 *Rufus:* It is easy for me to write these letters.

Rufus writes b (beta), t (tau), s (sigma) and u (upsilon).

2 *Rufus:* But it is difficult for me to write these letters.

Rufus writes zd (zeta), x (xi) and ps (psi).

3 *Demetrius:* Hooray, Rufus! You are working hard.

At last Rufus learns all the Greek letters.

4 Rufus was writing for a long time. Now he is tired.

5 *Demetrius:* Greece is beautiful. You will have to visit Greece, especially Delphi.

6 *Rufus:* Why is Delphi so famous?
Demetrius: Because the oracle at Delphi is well known.

7 *Demetrius:* I was visiting Delphi many years ago. I was consulting the oracle.

8 *Demetrius:* I was watching the Pythia.
Rufus: Who is the Pythia?
Demetrius: She is the famous priestess.

9 *Rufus:* What was the Pythia doing?
Demetrius: The Pythia was sitting on a tripod and she was chewing leaves.

10 *Demetrius:* The Pythia was uttering the responses of Apollo.
Rufus: It's a miracle! I also want to see the priestess!

Grasp the grammar

1 **facile est** (impersonal verb), **scrībere** (infinitive), **scrībit** (present tense)
2 **difficile est** (impersonal verb), **scrībere** (infinitive), **scrībit** (present tense)
3 **labōrās** (present tense), **discit** (present tense)
4 **scrībēbat** (imperfect tense), **est** (present tense)
5 **est** (present tense), **necesse erit** (impersonal verb), **vīsitāre** (infinitive)
6 **sunt** (present tense), **est** (present tense)
7 **vīsitābam** (imperfect tense), **cōnsulēbam** (imperfect tense)
8 **spectābam** (imperfect tense), **est** (*twice*, present tense)
9 **faciēbat** (imperfect tense), **sedēbat** (imperfect tense), **mandēbat** (imperfect tense)
10 **prōferēbat** (imperfect tense), **est** (present tense), **vidēre** (infinitive), **volō** (present tense)

Roman report: Delphi

- The **omphalos** or navel stone is in the splendid museum at Delphi.
- There were other oracles throughout Greece but the one at Delphi was the most important.

- Pilgrims came to Delphi during a period of more than 1,000 years. Those who are familiar with the terrain will appreciate the enormous achievement of actually reaching this very high, mountainous site.
- Pilgrims believed that they were communing with the god of prophecy, Apollo.
- The priestess had to be a woman over 50 and a virgin. Before uttering the prophecies, she had to purify herself in the Castalian spring.
- Some prophecies were notoriously ambiguous.
- Excavations at Delphi were begun by the French in the nineteenth century and are still continuing.
- Pupils may well need an explanation of **tripod** as a seat if they know the word in the context of photography or a laboratory. Point out the Greek roots of the word: **treis** (3) and **pous** [genitive – **podos**] (a foot).

Words to remember

Nouns
annus (m) year
nauta (m) sailor
nāvis (f) ship

Verbs
grātiās agere to thank
habitāre to live
legere to read
nāvigāre to sail
scrībere to write
sedēre to sit
vidēre to see

Adjectives
fessus/a/um tired
tūtus/a/um safe

Suggested activities

GEOGRAPHY
- Using an atlas, locate Delphi and York. Discuss methods of transport for making such a journey in Roman times.

ENGLISH
- Make a comparison between consulting the oracle at Delphi and the scene in chapter 7 where Flavia's twins had their horoscopes told. Is it appropriate/sensible/dangerous to try to discover the future? Comparisons could also be made with palmistry, newspaper horoscopes, etc., especially the unreliability of such methods of predicting the future. It may also be appropriate to discuss the dangers of ouija boards and seances.

ART
- Make a large copy of each of the bronze tablets.

Activity sheet answers

Note on 'breathings'

There was no letter h in the Greek alphabet. Instead, the Greeks used a symbol called a 'breathing'. If an 'h' sound was required before a word beginning with a vowel, they used a 'rough breathing', which looks like this ῾ (e.g. Ἑλλας). If no 'h' sound was required in a word that began with a vowel, they used a 'smooth breathing', which looks like this ᾿ (e.g. ἰδεα).

(There are seven vowels in Greek: alpha, epsilon, eta, iota, omicron, upsilon and omega.)

ACTIVITY SHEET XXX

Proper names		General words	
1	Heracles	**11**	drama
2	Odysseus	**12**	hippopotamus
3	Persephone	**13**	idea
4	Alexander	**14**	orchestra
5	Demetrius	**15**	catastrophe
6	Cyclops	**16**	dilemma
7	Hellas (Greece)	**17**	rhododendron
8	Athens	**18**	rhinoceros
9	Parthenon	**19**	asthma
10	Pegasus	**20**	pneumonia

9 Martius
Wonderful days!

■ **subject matter:** naming a baby; hunting ■ **materials:** activity sheets XXXIII–XXXVI
■ **grammar content:** imperfect tense of **esse** (to be); compound verbs

Picture story

The twins are named (pp. 63–64)

1 *Lepidina:* On the eighth day, friends and relations were coming to the house.

2 *Lepidina:* It was the day of purification. Gaius was holding his daughter.

3 *Lepidina:* Gaius was sprinkling water on his daughter.
Gaius: Your name is Gaia Charisa.

4 *Lepidina:* Everyone was giving presents. Everyone was very happy.

5 Rufus wanted to give bronze animals.
Lepidina: But it was dangerous because Charisa was small.

6 *Lepidina:* On the next day everyone was returning to the house. Again they were giving toys.

7 *Lepidina:* Gaius was sprinkling water on his son.
Gaius: Your name is Gaius Castor.

8 *Lepidina:* The two babies were wearing lockets.

9 *Rufus:* A wooden sword was my gift.
Pandora: You were kind.

10 *Lepidina:* The days were marvellous.
Pandora: I love babies! Perhaps one day I shall be a mother . . .

NB The name Charisa is from the Greek word χαρις (**charis**) meaning 'grace'. Castor is one of the twins from Classical mythology, known as the Dioscuri, Castor and Pollux. They were also star constellations that guided sailors.

Grasp the grammar

Imperfect tense verbs in the picture story:

Pic. 1	**veniēbant**	they were coming
Pic. 2	**tenēbat**	he was holding
Pic. 3	**spargēbat**	he was sprinkling
Pic. 4	**dabant**	they were giving
Pic. 5	**volēbat**	he wanted (*lit.* he was wanting)
Pic. 6	**reveniēbant**	they were returning
	dabant	they were giving
Pic. 7	**spargēbat**	he was sprinkling
Pic. 8	**gerēbant**	they were wearing

Examples of the imperfect tense of the verb 'to be':

Pic. 2	**erat**	it was
Pic. 4	**erant**	they were
Pic. 5	**erat**	it was
	erat	she was
Pic. 9	**erat**	it was
	erās	you were
Pic. 10	**erant**	they were

Latin roots

1 <u>octet</u> from **octō**, the number eight. A group of eight musicians.

2 <u>infantile</u> from **īnfāns**, a baby, or young child. Childish behaviour.

3 <u>tenacious</u> from **tenēre**, to hold. Holding tightly.

Roman report: welcoming a baby

The seven days after the birth of a baby were spent preparing for the day of purification (**diēs lūstricus**). As with modern naming ceremonies, this would be an opportunity for a family gathering and a time for celebration and thanksgiving for the safe arrival of the baby. Various minor Roman deities were thought to guard newborn babies.

Although freeborn citizens normally had three names, many people in Britain had only two names and sometimes just one.

Picture story

Time to go home (pp. 67–68)

1. The whole family was returning home.

   Lepidina: Goodbye, Flavia! Take care of your beautiful twins!

2. *Candidus:* Flavius and his friend, called Brocchus, were leaving for the hunt. I was also there.

3. *Pandora:* What were you doing?
   Candidus: I was carrying hunting spears and nets.

4. *Candidus:* We were riding to the woods. Many dogs were there with us.

5. *Candidus:* The segosi were smelling/sniffing out the hares and were howling.

6. *Candidus:* The vertragi were running very quickly. These dogs were marvellous.

7. *Candidus:* A very large boar was in the woods.

8. *Candidus:* Flavius and Brocchus were searching for the boar, but in vain.

9. *Candidus:* At last seven partridges, five hares and one deer were dead.

10. *Flavius:* It was an excellent day.
    Brocchus: Yes. Silvanus was with us.

Grasp the grammar

Imperfect tense verbs in the picture story:

Pic. 1	**reveniēbat**	it was returning
Pic. 2	**discēdēbant**	they were leaving
	aderam	I was there
Pic. 3	**faciēbās**	you were doing
	portābam	I was carrying
Pic. 4	**equitābāmus**	we were riding
	aderant	they were there
Pic. 5	**olfaciēbant**	they were sniffing
	ululābant	they were howling
Pic. 6	**currēbant**	they were running
	erant	they were
Pic. 7	**erat**	there was
Pic. 8	**petēbant**	they were searching for
Pic. 9	**erant**	they were
Pic. 10	**erat**	it was
	aderat	he was there

Compounds of the verb 'to be':

1. he/she/it was here
2. we were under
3. they were able
4. we were surviving
5. you (sing.) were away
6. I was in
7. you (pl.) were here
8. he/she/it was in charge
9. we were away
10. he was able

Latin roots

1. canine from **canis**, a dog.
2. amicably from **amīcus**, a friend. In a friendly way.
3. imports and exports from **portāre**, to carry, plus the two prepositions **in** (in) and **ex** (out). Goods brought into or sent out of a country.
4. curator from **cūrāre**, to care for.
5. frustrated from **frūstrā**, in vain.

Roman report: hunting

- Brocchus is Aelius Brocchus, a friend of Flavius, whose wife Claudia Severa invited Lepidina to her birthday party in the first chapter of the first *Minimus* book. The four seem to have been good friends; there are a number of letters between both the men and the women. Apart from the famous birthday invitation, Brocchus invited Flavius and Lepidina to join them to celebrate New Year. Brocchus seems to have been the prefect of the fort at Briga, which may have been modern Kirkbride. At any rate, it cannot have been too far from Vindolanda. Brocchus dedicated an altar to Diana while commanding a cavalry regiment in Pannonia. We assume from this that he went to the Dacian wars and was promoted to command cavalry. He is one of the few 'Vindolanda names' which appear elsewhere.
- There is an altar from Bollihope Common, Co. Durham, dedicated to Silvanus. It commemorates the successful killing of 'a boar of outstanding size' which others had been unable to kill.
- The geographer Strabo mentions Britain as a good source of hunting dogs. The Vindolanda tablets make it clear that hunting was enormously popular in the north of Britain at this time. It seems not unlikely that, although Flavius has moved to Eboracum and has left the army, he and Brocchus would take any opportunity to pursue their favourite hobby.
- Arrian gives detailed descriptions of various hunting dogs. The two breeds in the story (segosi and vertragi) are both mentioned in the Vindolanda tablets. The segosi were known for their ability to scent animal tracks but they were also ugly and noisy. Arrian says: 'Among the Celts there is a famous comparison with roadside beggars because of their mournful and miserable voice . . .' 'The segosi are skilled at scenting animal tracks. They bark or howl on the trail uncontrollably when they have found the scent. As to their appearance, they are shaggy and ugly, the purer the breed, the uglier.'

  The vertragi were famous for their speed. Arrian had a much-loved vertragus bitch called Eagerness. He describes the breed like this: 'The really fast Celtic dogs are called vertragi. There is nothing finer to look at than the shape and appearance of the best bred of these dogs.'

Words to remember

Nouns
diēs (m) day
gladius (m) sword
nōmen (n) name
vīlla (f) house

Verbs
abesse to be absent
adesse to be present
amāre to love/to like
dare to give
esse to be
petere to seek/make for
portāre to carry
posse to be able
venīre to come

Adverbs
fortasse perhaps
ōlim once upon a time (past) *or* at some time (future)
postrīdiē on the next day

Suggested activities

RS

- Discuss the Roman customs associated with birth and the naming day. Compare them with a modern baptism or other naming ceremony from religions represented in the class. Class could discuss the significance of the various rituals. Find parallels and differences. Pupils who have recently attended such an event might do a short talk to the class.
- Discussion about the Roman **bulla** might lead to a broader discussion about the differences between religion, tradition and superstition.

ART

- Paint or sketch the two different types of hunting dog.
- Make a classroom frieze, drawing all the animals that you have met so far in both *Minimus* books. Label each animal in Latin.

ENGLISH

- **Debate:** the second story might lead to a debate on fox hunting. Whatever the pupils' views on hunting, they should know how popular it was among the Romans. Pliny writes to a friend (Book 2, No. 8) and is envious of him because he has time to read, fish and hunt. Pliny, on the other hand, 'sees his work stretching out farther and farther every day . . .'.

- In the first story, pupils met the Latin for the numbers two (**duo**) and eight (**octō**). In the second story they met one (**ūnus**), five (**quīnque**) and seven (**septem**).
  Using the following list of the numbers from one to ten, have a class competition to see who can produce the most English derivatives from the numbers. Alternatively, divide the class into small groups; each group picks a Latin number from some numbered cards (see e.g. activity sheet XXXIV) and then has to research that number and collect derivatives from it. The results could be produced as a poster.

1 ūnus/ūna/ūnum
2 duo/duae/duo
3 trēs/trēs/tria
4 quattuor
5 quīnque
6 sex
7 septem
8 octō
9 novem
10 decem

NB Only one, two and three have variable endings.

Activity sheet answers

ACTIVITY SHEET XXXVI

Teachers are advised to enlarge the snap cards for this game.

10 Aprīlis
Comings and goings

■ **subject matter:** slavery ■ **materials:** activity sheets XXXVII–XXXIX
■ **grammar content:** participles

Picture story

Barates comes to buy (pp. 71–72)

1 *Barates:* I am lonely. I am miserable. I want to buy a new slave girl.

Barates looks for Flavius.

2 Flavius, called to the main room, hurries as quickly as possible.

Flavius: Hello, friend! What do you want?

3 *Barates:* Hello! I want to buy Pandora. How much is she?

4 *Flavius:* Aha! Candidus! Look for Pandora!

Candidus, sent by his master, hurries out of the main room.

5 Pandora, led into the main room, looks at Barates. Pandora smiles.

6 *Flavius:* Pandora is hard-working. Pandora is an excellent hairdresser and sings sweetly. Therefore Pandora is expensive/dear.

7 *Flavius:* I want two hundred denarii. Is that all right?

Barates: That's all right.

8 *Flavius:* Excellent! Corinthus, prepare a tablet!

Corinthus, ordered by his master, writes the terms on the tablet!

9 Pandora, bought by Barates, is now anxious.

Corinthus & Candidus: Don't be afraid! Barates is kind.

10 But Corinthus and Candidus are very unhappy.

Grasp the grammar

Participles:

Pic. 2	**vocātus**	called (masculine)
Pic. 8	**iussus**	ordered (masculine)
Pic. 9	**ēmpta**	bought (feminine)

Latin roots

1 mission from **mittere**, to send (the participle is **missus**).

2 novelty from **novus**, new.

3 spectacles from **spectāre**, to watch. Note also **spectāculum** (n), a show or spectacle and **spectātor**, a spectator.

4 deride from **dērīdēre**, to mock or laugh at (a compound of **rīdēre**, to laugh or smile).

5 induction from **indūcere**, to lead in. **dūcere** and its compounds have many derivatives, such as *production*, *produce*, *reproduce*, *introduction*, *aqueduct* and *viaduct*. Pupils could illustrate this verb and all its compounds with a suitable image, for example a pipe (or 'duct') leading from Latin to English.

NB Activity sheet XXXVIII asks pupils to find as many derivatives as they can from four Latin participles (**scrīptus**, **ductus**, **missus** and **positus**).

Background information: the slave trade

There was already a slave trade in Britain before the Romans invaded. Cicero, writing to his friend Atticus in 54 BC, says: 'The outcome of the British campaign is eagerly awaited . . . but we now know that there is not a trace of silver in the island and that the only hope of plunder is slaves – and I don't think you're expecting to find any literary or musical geniuses amongst them!' (*ad Atticum*, iv, 16.7)

The geographer Strabo also lists slaves among Britain's exports: 'The island produces corn, cattle, gold, silver, iron. All these are exported, along with hides, slaves and dogs useful for hunting.' (*Geographia*, iv, 5 1–2)

Slaves could be bought either by private arrangement or at a slave market. In a market, slaves would be displayed on a platform. Placards around their necks stated their name, age, nationality and skills. In addition, Pliny the Elder tells us: 'The cheapest sort of chalk is the one we traditionally use to mark the victory line in races at the Circus and to whiten the feet of imported slaves at auctions.' (*Natural History*, XXXV) In the absence of any reference to this practice in Britain, it has not been included in the picture story; nevertheless it may well have happened in Britain too and pupils will enjoy this detail.

As well as local slaves, it would be quite normal to see many foreign slaves for sale in the markets. Both neck and foot chains have been found in Britain.

How much?
It is pretty well impossible to give modern equivalents for the price of a slave. It seems that female slaves cost less than males. Young, energetic slaves would cost more, as would literate and/or skilled slaves, such as Pandora. In AD 129 we have an instance of a female slave, aged 25, who was sold for 1200 sesterces. This equates to 300 denarii – a year's pay for a legionary soldier. Barates is a successful merchant so he can afford a high price for Pandora. At 200 denarii, she is an expensive investment – quite how good an investment will be seen in the final chapter!

Picture story
Slave girl wanted! (pp. 74–75)

1 *Lepidina:* I must have a new slave girl.
Flavius: We must hurry to the market.

Flavius and Lepidina go out as quickly as possible.

2 Flavius sees slaves, bound/tied up in chains.

3 Lepidina sees slave girls, set up on a platform.

4 The slaves and slave girls are wearing placards.

5 Lepidina reads the words written on the placards.

6 *Slave-dealer:* This slave girl is Spanish. She dances excellently!

7 *Slave-dealer:* This slave girl is Greek. She knows the Latin language!

8 *Slave-dealer:* Look! This slave girl is German. She cooks skilfully and sings sweetly and . . .
Lepidina: Enough! The German slave girl pleases me/I like the German slave girl.

9 Flavius and the slave-dealer agree a price. The slave girl, handed over to Flavius, smiles nervously/timidly.
They return home.

10 *Flavius:* Candidus! Corinthus! Rufus! This is the new slave girl. This is Trifosa.

Corinthus & Candidus: Aha! Life is better . . .

- Ask pupils to think about why Lepidina chooses the German slave girl. There may be many possible reasons but remind pupils that Flavius and his family are Batavians and come from the German/Dutch border. Lepidina will be delighted to have a slave girl from home who may well speak her native language.
- In pictures 6, 7 and 8 pupils may need help with a suppressed subject: clearly the slave girl must be the subject in the second sentence in each case, but the word **ancilla** is not given. This is common practice in Latin and it is worth drawing pupils' attention to it. The rule is that if a new subject is not mentioned, in the

nominative case, assume that the subject is the same as in the previous sentence.

Grasp the grammar

If appropriate for your pupils, point out that a participle, like an adjective, must agree in **case** as well as gender and number with the noun it describes.

In picture 2, for example, the slaves (**servōs**) are in the accusative case, because the slaves are the object of the sentence; so the participle (**vīnctōs**) is also in the accusative.

Participles:

Pic. 3 **positās** – describes **ancillās** (feminine, plural, accusative)

Pic. 5 **scrīpta** – describes **verba** (neuter, plural, accusative)

Pic. 9 **trādita** – describes **ancilla** (feminine, singular, nominative)

Words to remember

Noun
vīta (f) life

Verbs
ēmere to buy
festīnāre to hurry

Participles
missus sent
positus positioned
trāditus handed over
vīnctus tied up

Adjectives
melior/melior/melius better
novus/a/um new
sōlus/a/um alone/lonely

Suggested activities

DRAMA

- Hold a slave market. Write a short script in English. Use as many details as possible from the picture story (e.g. platform, placards, canny slave-dealer, a scribe to write down the terms of an agreement, price, bargaining, chalk on the feet).
- Work in groups. One pupil plays Barates, one Pandora, one Candidus, one Lepidina and one Rufus. Write and perform a dialogue in which each character examines what the sale of Pandora means to him or her.

HISTORY/PSHE

- Discuss the Roman slave system. Pupils could research the slave trade in Britain, America, etc. and find modern parallels (could include a discussion of the minimum wage, or children working in sweat shops in developing countries).

Activity sheet answers

ACTIVITY SHEET XXXIX

For further practice with the Greek alphabet, pupils could write the goddesses' names in Greek letters:

Hera – Ἡρα

Athene – Ἀθηνη

Artemis – Ἀρτεμις

11 Māius
Timber into stone

■ **subject matter:** construction work at Eboracum ■ **materials:** activity sheets XL–XLIII
■ **grammar content:** revision – parts of the verb

Picture story
The new headquarters (pp. 77–78)

1 *Flavius:* Look! The dockers are carrying the stones that were cut in the quarry.

2 *Flavius:* Then the labourers unload the stones which were dragged in wagons/which they have dragged in wagons.

3 *Flavius:* The architect and I are designing the new headquarters. It is a very big building.

4 *Flavius:* Meanwhile the surveyors are inspecting the ground.

5 *Rufus:* What is this machine?
Flavius: It is a groma. The surveyors are checking the plan.

6 *Flavius:* Look! The labourers are levelling the ground.

7 *Flavius:* Look! The sculptors are carving columns.

8 *Rufus:* But the labourers are stopping. They are lazy! They are drinking beer!

9 *Flavius:* Work hard!

10 The labourers, ordered by Flavius, reluctantly begin to work.

Grasp the grammar

Participles:

Pic. 1 **secta**, from **secāre** (to cut), agrees with **saxa** (neuter plural)

Pic. 2 **tracta**, from **trahere** (to drag), agrees with **saxa** (neuter plural)

Pic. 10 **iussī**, from **iubēre** (to order), agrees with **operāriī** (masculine plural)

Infinitive: labōrāre (to work) in picture 10

Imperative: labōrāte, plural imperative from **labōrāre** (to work), in picture 9

Latin roots

1 dissecting from **dissecāre**, to cut.
2 diligently from **dīligenter**, hard/carefully.
3 incipient from **incipere**, to begin.
4 Mediterranean from **medius**, middle and **terra**, earth. People in the ancient world believed that the Mediterranean was at the centre of the earth.

Roman report: construction work at Eboracum

There are obvious problems in attempting to ascertain what the Roman headquarters building, and indeed the whole military fortress, looked like. After this early Roman period, it was built on not only by later Romans but also by the Normans and in medieval times. If at all possible, teachers are urged to visit York Minster and the undercroft in particular. This houses all the visible remains of the early fortress. It also has an excellent model of York through the ages which uses different colours to make clear the Norman, Saxon and Roman remains, which are superimposed on each other in many places.

By the beginning of the second century, Roman forts and fortresses had acquired a fairly standardised shape, so we can reconstruct with some confidence the probable layout of the fortress at York. Archaeologists can tell that the headquarters was at the centre of the fortress and that it was colonnaded on three sides. Moreover, one column base remains and from this we can work out the dimensions of the colonnade. It has been calculated that it was over 20 metres high. The military headquarters was the administrative centre for the whole legion. There seems to have been a shrine where the standards of the legion were stored and beneath the building was a treasury where the soldiers' pay was kept.

To set out straight lines for the roads and buildings, Roman surveyors used an instrument called a **grōma**. This was a vertical pole with a flat cross on the top. From the arms of the cross hung four plumb-lines, which were weighted with lead or bronze. The surveyor's assistant would hold up a pole at a distance and would move from right to left until the surveyor (**agrimēnsor**) was able to see it in line with two of the plumb-lines. (There is an illustration of a groma on activity sheet XLI.)

Picture story
Some builders are better than others . . . (pp. 80–81)

1. The wooden fortress is destroyed. Now some soldiers are building a fortress made of stone.
2. All the Brigantes are standing in astonishment.
   Brigantes: The fortress is solid.
3. Other soldiers are building a very big gate.
4. The soldiers have a drawing, depicted on a tablet.
5. An excellent sculptor, ordered by Flavius, begins to carve the inscription.
6. The soldiers are lifting very big stones. The Brigantes are looking at the amazing crane.
7. *Flavius:* Watch out, soldiers! Oh dear! The stones are not in their proper place.
8. Suddenly the soldiers drop a stone. There is a huge crash.
9. *Rufus:* Look! There's a little mouse, almost struck by the stone.
10. Rufus saves the mouse.
    Rufus: Hooray! The mouse is alive.

Grasp the grammar

Pic. 1 **dēlētum** (neuter, agrees with **castellum**) from **dēlēre**, to destroy

Pic. 4 **pictam** (feminine, agrees with **dēscrīptiōnem**) from **pingere**, to paint/draw

Pic. 5 **iussus** (masculine, agrees with **sculptor**) from **iubēre**, to order

Pic. 9 **percussus** (masculine, agrees with **mūs**) from **percutere**, to strike/hit

Latin roots

1. percussion from **percutere**, to hit. Instruments that need to be hit (triangle, xylophone, etc.).
2. lapidary from **lapis**, stone. Works with stone.
3. edifice from **aedificāre**, to build and/or **aedificium**, a building.
4. Picts from **pingere**, to paint/draw (the participle is **pictus**).

Greek myth

The myth is from Homer's *Odyssey*, Book IX.

Words to remember

Nouns
porta (f) gate
prīncipia (n pl) headquarters

Verbs
aedificāre to build
bibere to drink
habēre to have
īnspicere to inspect
servāre to save
stāre to stand

Adjectives
invītus/a/um unwilling
parvus/a/um small
vīvus/a/um alive

Suggested activities

ENGLISH

- Imagine that you are visiting the building site in Eboracum as a TV or radio reporter. Interview Celts, soldiers and the architect about progress. There might be some disgruntled Celts who don't want the Romans there, but others might see the Roman invasion as bringing much-needed amenities. Report back for the local news.

GEOGRAPHY

- Research what types of stone were available to the soldiers. Where were the local quarries? How would the stone have been transported? How long would a single journey from the quarry to the site take?

MATHS

Roman measurements	
lībra	a Roman pound = 327.45 grammes It was divided into 12 **ūnciae**.
sextārius	a measure of liquids and of corn = just under a pint (0.96 of a pint)
pēs	a Roman foot = 29.46 centimetres It was divided into 12 **ūnciae** (inches).
mīlle passūs	a Roman mile = 1536 metres (132 yards short of an English mile)

- Measure your classroom in Roman feet. Convert the distance from home to school into Roman miles. Convert a recipe into Roman weights. (Activity sheet XL gives more ideas for measuring activities.)

ICT

- Plot the data from the measuring exercise on to a computer database or graph.

DT

- Use activity sheet XLI to construct a groma.

Activity sheet answers

ACTIVITY SHEET XLII

1	**prīncipia**	headquarters
2	**vallum**	rampart
3	**fossa**	ditch
4	**officīna**	workshop
5	**balnea**	baths
6	**praetōrium**	commander's house
7	**valētūdinārium**	hospital
8	**via Decumāna**	the main streets of the fortress
9	**via Prīncipālis**	
10	**via Praetōria**	
11	**horrea**	granaries
12	**contubernia**	barracks
13	**latrīna**	lavatory

ACTIVITY SHEET XLIII

1. Look, it's Minimus!/Here is Minimus!
2. Look, it's Minima!/Here is Minima!
3. Minimus watches Minima.
4. Minima blushes.
5. Minima watches Minimus.
6. Minima carries cheese.
7. Minima drops the cheese!
8. Minimus helps Minima.
9. Minimus and Minima eat the cheese.

12 Iūnius
All change for Pandora

■ **subject matter:** freedom; betrothal ■ **materials:** activity sheets XLIV–XLVI
■ **grammar content:** revision

Picture story
Freedom! (pp. 84–85)

1 Barates invites the family to dinner.

Barates: Enter! You are very welcome!

2 *Barates:* I want to free Pandora. Pandora! Sit with me!

3 *Barates:* I want you to be witnesses. I am setting Pandora free.

Family: Yes. Hooray!

4 Pandora, who has been made a freedwoman, is very happy.

5 *Lepidina:* Trifosa! Pandora is now a freedwoman. You must serve the food.

6 Trifosa nervously carries in the food.

7 Suddenly Trifosa drops the food.

Trifosa: Oh no! There is mess everywhere!

8 Trifosa is crying. Corinthus and Candidus are helping Trifosa.

9 *Pandora:* Don't cry! I was also nervous. You will be an excellent slave girl.

10 Meanwhile, Vibrissa, Minimus and Minima are eating the food.

Revise the grammar

(The number in brackets indicates which picture the word appears in.)

Personal pronouns: **vōs** (3), **ego** (9), **tū** (9). Pupils may also come up with **mihi** (2) and **tibi** (5): if appropriate, attention should be drawn to these dative forms.

Singular imperative: **sedē!** (2)

Plural imperative: **intrāte!** (1)

Negative imperative: **nōlī lacrimāre!** (9)

Impersonal verbs: **mihi placet** (2), **necesse est** (5)

Infinitives: **līberāre** (2), **esse** (3), **offerre** (5), **lacrimāre** (9)

Participle: **facta** (4)

Compound verb: one of the following – **offerre** (5), **importat** (6), **adiuvant** (8)

Imperfect: **eram** (9)

Latin roots

1 edible from **edere**, to eat. Good to eat.
2 testify from **testis**, a witness. To give evidence.
3 squalid from **squālor**, mess or **squālidus**, dirty.
4 liberty from **līberāre**, to free. Note also **līberta** (a freedwoman), **lībertus** (a freedman) and **lībertās** (freedom).

Roman report: freeing slaves

As Barates is a family friend, it is envisaged that he uses an informal method of freeing Pandora.

Picture story
The party continues (pp. 87–88)

1 Candidus and Trifosa are cooking another dinner.

Candidus: You cook very well.

Trifosa blushes.

2 *Barates:* I want you to be witnesses. I want Pandora to be my wife.

3 *Barates:* Pandora. Look! This ring is for you.

Barates hands over a bronze ring.

4 *Pandora:* Thank you very much. How kind you are!

5 Pandora immediately puts the ring on her third finger.

Barates: I am your fiancé and you are my fiancée.

6 *Barates:* And this is another present.

Barates hands over a fan.

7 *Pandora:* How lucky I am!

Corinthus & Candidus (whisper): No! How lucky Barates is!

8 *Flavius:* We must drink a toast. More wine!

Everyone: Congratulations! Hooray!

9 Trifosa is dancing very well. Corinthus and Candidus are smiling.

10 *Minimus:* Minima! Let's party!

But Vibrissa is sleeping.

Latin roots

1 Italian – *grazie*, Spanish – *gracias*

2 *le doigt annulaire*

Roman report: betrothal

Betrothals were so common that Pliny includes them among the many trifles that crowd his day: 'It is extraordinary how, if one takes a single day spent in Rome, one can give a more or less accurate account of it, but scarcely any account at all of several days put together. If you ask anyone what he did that day, the answer would be: "I was present at a coming of age ceremony, a betrothal, or a wedding . . ."' (*Letters*, 1:9)

Our evidence for such ceremonies, as for many aspects of life dealt with in *Minimus*, tends to be descriptions of what happened in Rome itself. Nevertheless it seems more than likely that people in the provinces deliberately imitated the customs of the capital. Indeed Tacitus corroborates this in the *Agricola*: 'So it was that a people who had at first rejected the Latin language became keen to speak it fluently. In the same way, our dress became popular and the toga came into fashion. Gradually, the Britons were led astray. They were tempted into adopting such vices as porticoes, baths and sumptuous dinner parties. The uneducated natives spoke of such novelties as "civilisation" when really it was part of their enslavement!' (*Agricola*, Ch. 21)

Words to remember

Nouns	Adverb
ānulus (m) ring	**intereā** meanwhile
līberta (f) freedwoman	**Idiom**
uxor (f) wife	**mēcum** with me
Verb	
trādere to hand over	

Suggested activities

DISCUSSION

- Is Pandora really lucky? Pupils will probably focus on the very different ages and backgrounds of Pandora and Barates, and perhaps on the fact that Barates had been Pandora's master. However, this is probably Pandora's best chance of escaping from slavery into security and a family of her own. You could mention the fact that manumission was quite common in the Roman world in contrast with other periods of history.

HISTORY/DISCUSSION

- Research and discuss the position of women in the ancient world.

Photocopiable activity sheets

Meet the family now

Name: ____________________ Date: __________

Colour in and label the family group. If you remember the characters from the first *Minimus* book, do you think they have changed in five years? Who is the new member of the family on the right? You'll find out in chapter 3.

The horse's head-dress

Name: ______________________ Date: ____________

Complete and colour this picture of the head-dress (**chamfron**) that Flavius's horse wears in the parade.

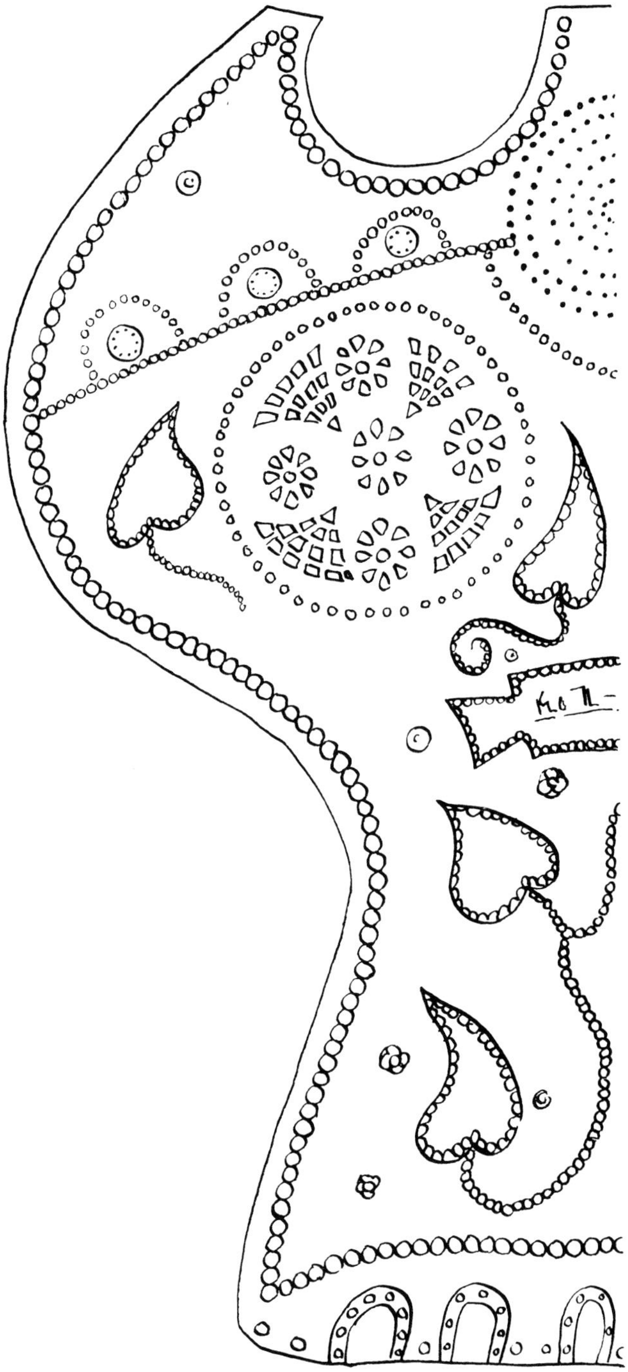

Practice makes perfect

Name: ______________________ Date: ____________

The present tense

Translate these sentences into English.
There are some verbs below to help you. Remember that you can handle hundreds of Latin verbs now that you know six endings!

Example: **appropinquāmus** means "we approach".

1 rōdit ____________________
2 mūgīmus ____________________
3 serpitis ____________________
4 conculcat ____________________
5 stertunt ____________________
6 rōdunt ____________________
7 conculcās ____________________
8 balbūtīs ____________________
9 balbūtīmus ____________________
10 serpō ____________________
11 mūgiō ____________________
12 stertis ____________________

rōdō	I nibble	**mūgiō**	I moo	**serpō**	I crawl
conculcō	I trample	**stertō**	I snore	**balbūtiō**	I stammer

The verb "to be"

Using the information in chapter 1, write the Latin for:

1 we are ____________________
2 she is ____________________
3 I am ____________________
4 you (*sing.*) are ____________________
5 they are ____________________
6 you (*pl.*) are ____________________
7 I am Flavius. ____________________
8 You are Pandora. ____________________
9 We are Minimus and Vibrissa. ____________________
10 They are soldiers. ____________________
11 You are Candidus and Corinthus. ____________________
12 She is Lepidina. ____________________

The verb "to be" in different Romance languages

Name: ____________________ Date: __________

The family of Romance languages are those which developed from Latin. Here is the verb "to be" written out in Latin and in five Romance languages spoken in countries that were once part of the Roman Empire.

Latin	French	Italian	Spanish	Portuguese	Romanian
sum	je suis	io sono	yo soy	eu sou	eu sunt
es	tu es	tu sei	tú eres	tu és	tu esti
est	il est	lui è	él es	ele é	el este
sumus	nous sommes	noi siamo	nosotros somos	nós somos	noi suntem
estis	vous êtes	voi siete	vosotros sois	vós sois	voi sunteti
sunt	ils sont	loro sono	ellos son	eles são	ei sunt

How would these six characters introduce themselves in their own language? Research their national flags and colour them in. (The Roman flag might be red with crossed gold lightning bolts, like a legionary's shield.)

Iulius's journey to Dacia

Name:____________________ Date:__________

Which route do you think Iulius would have taken from Vindolanda to Dacia? Draw a dotted line to represent his journey. Using the internet and books on the Roman Empire, research sea ports and major road networks to find clues.

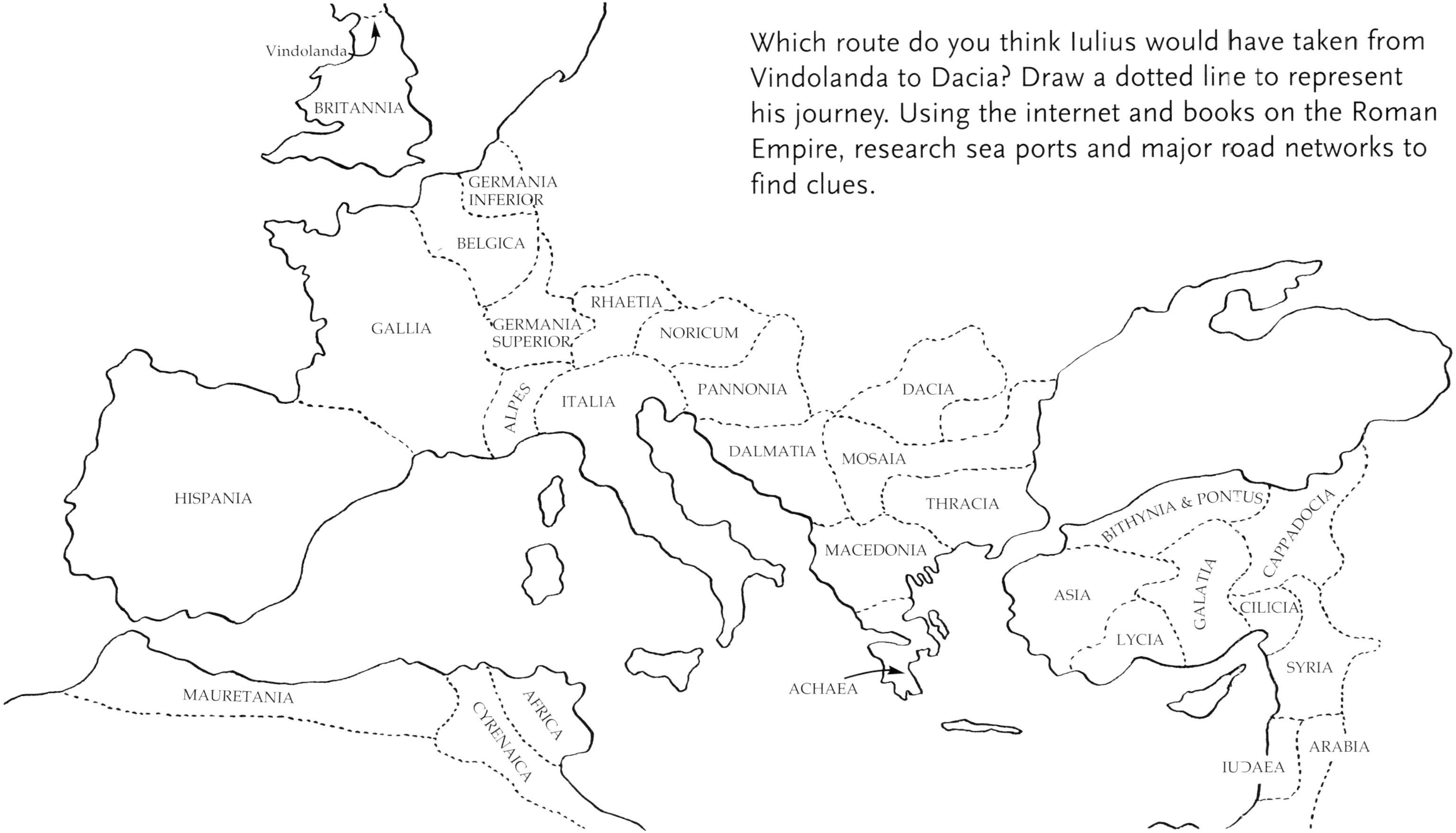

VI

Trajan's Column

Name: ____________________ Date: __________

The emperor Trajan commissioned a huge stone column in Rome. It was decorated with a continuous spiral sculpture commemorating his victorious campaigns in Dacia. This drawing represents one part of the sculpture. Study the drawing and comment on what is happening.

What's in Iulius's pack?

Name: ____________________ Date: __________

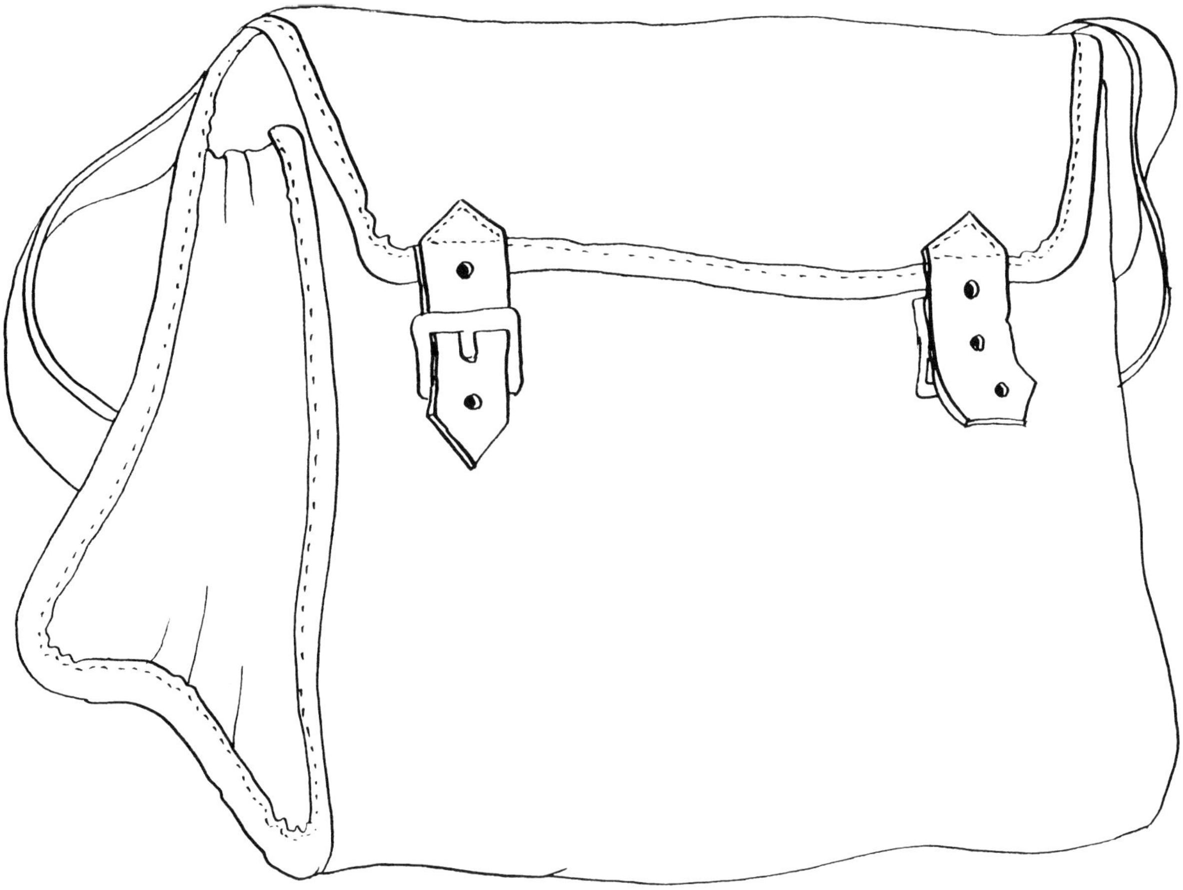

Here's a list of items that might have been in a legionary's pack when he was on the march. Which ones belong in the pack and which were not available to a Roman soldier? Put a tick or a cross next to each item. When your teacher has checked your answers, draw the correct items in the pack for Iulius to take to Dacia.

1 soap
2 tin of sardines
3 food pan
4 grain for porridge
5 socks
6 spade or pick
7 wooden stakes
8 mobile phone
9 salt
10 woollen hat
11 letter from home
12 water bottle
13 photo of family
14 dried fruit
15 folding knife
16 chocolate bar

Odysseus and the Sirens

Name: ____________________ Date: __________

Create your own cartoon version of the story.

The Sirens had women's heads and birds' bodies. They lured sailors to die on the rocks with their irresistible song.

Odysseus had to sail past them on his way home from the Trojan War.

He was curious to hear their song but he didn't want to die! He came up with a cunning plan.

He made his crew stuff their ears with beeswax to protect them from the Sirens' song.

Then Odysseus's crew tied him firmly to the mast and rowed towards the Sirens' rock.

The song was so lovely that Odysseus struggled desperately to jump overboard.

He screamed at his men to untie him but they couldn't hear his orders.

The men rowed frantically until they were safely out of earshot of the deadly song.

The Sirens were furious – Odysseus had heard their song and survived!

Towns of Roman Britain

Name: ______________________ Date: ____________

Identify these towns in Roman Britain, giving either their Latin name or the modern equivalent.

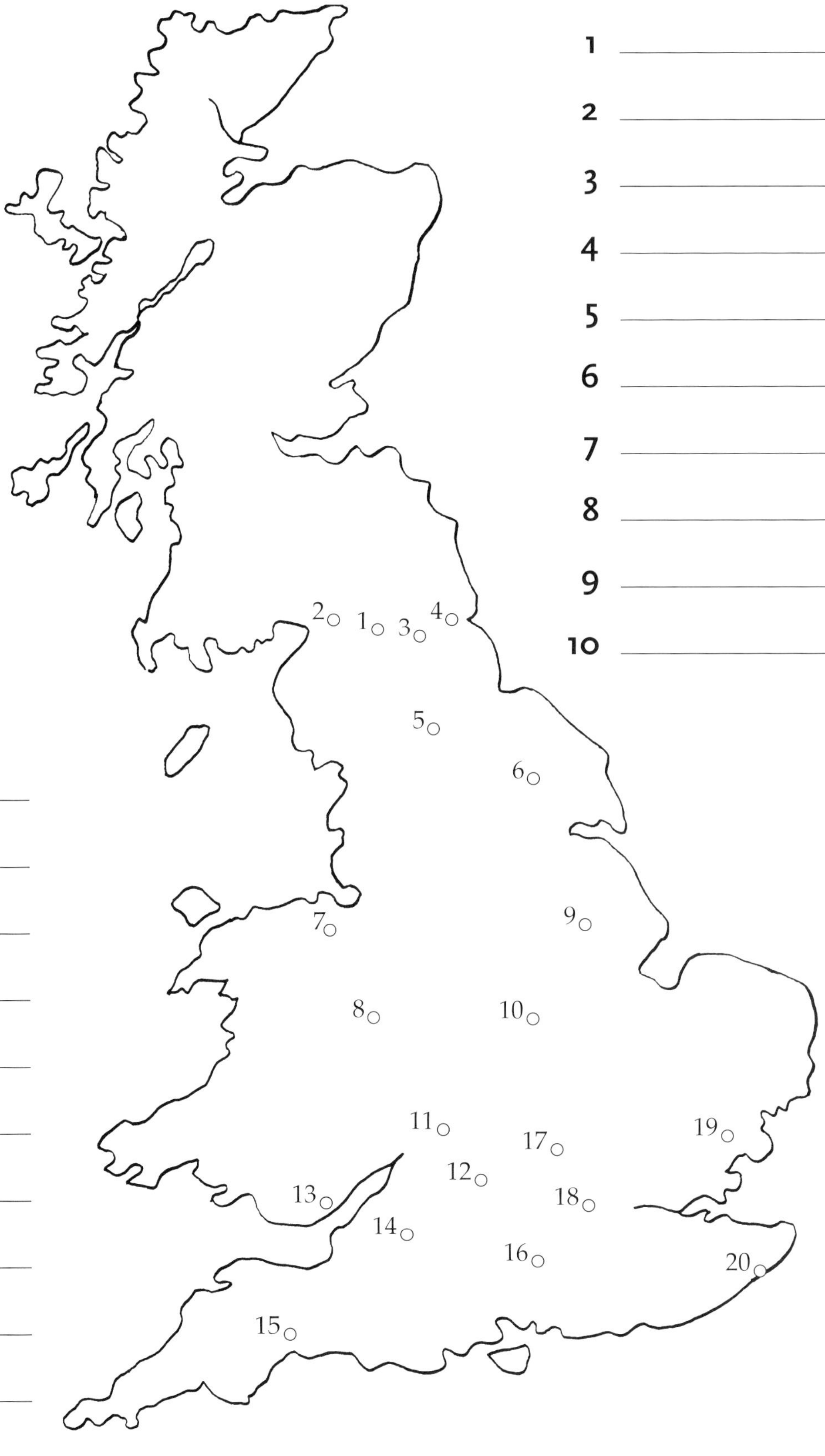

1 ____________________

2 ____________________

3 ____________________

4 ____________________

5 ____________________

6 ____________________

7 ____________________

8 ____________________

9 ____________________

10 ____________________

11 ____________________

12 ____________________

13 ____________________

14 ____________________

15 ____________________

16 ____________________

17 ____________________

18 ____________________

19 ____________________

20 ____________________

Happy Verb Families!

Name: ______________________ Date: ___________

Each family is made up of a verb in the present tense, an infinitive verb, an English translation and an English derivation. Cut out the card set and play (in groups of three or more) according to the usual Happy Families rules.

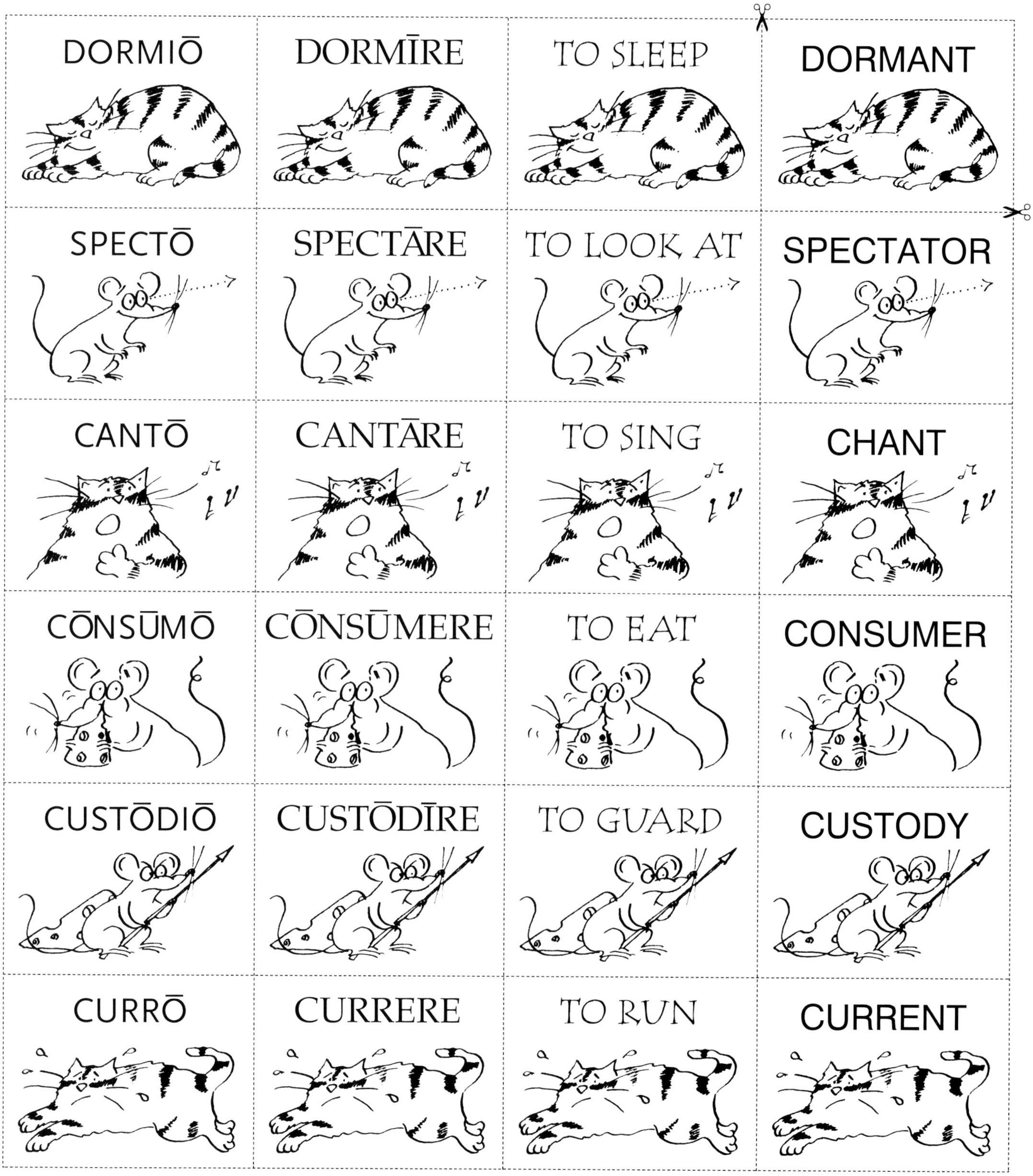

XI

Name: ____________________ Date: __________

You will need a dice and some glass nuggets or other counters.

Road transport

Name: ____________________ Date: __________

Write the correct Latin name in each box. Suggest what type of journey might be appropriate to each form of transport.

1

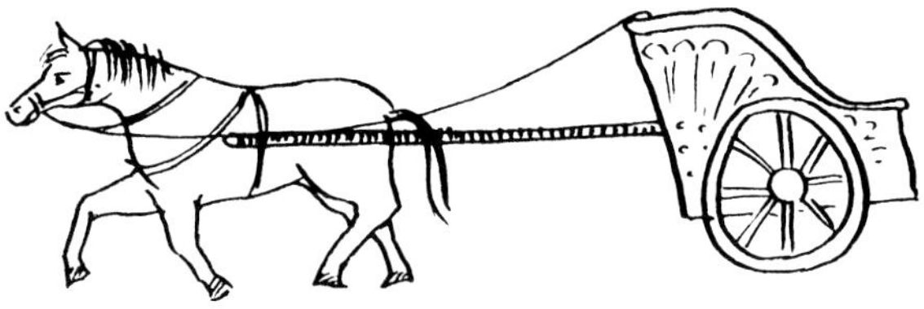

2

3

4

5

6

asinus	**lectīca**	**currus**
plaustrum	**equus**	**ambulō**

The Labours of Heracles

Name: ____________________ Date: __________

Research and illustrate the twelve labours of Heracles in the boxes below.

The lion with invulnerable skin	The Hydra	The deer with golden hooves
The giant boar	The mad Cretan bull	The stables of King Augeas
The cranes with bronze feathers	The man-eating mares	The Amazon Queen's belt
The cattle of Geryon, the three-bodied man	The apples of the Hesperides	Cerberus, the three-headed dog from Hell

Group project: make a Hydra

Name: ____________________ Date: ____________

You will need: modelling wire or untwisted wire coathangers; stuffing; rubber bands; red, green and white felt; old tights or stockings; green PVA or spray paint; foil; blue or green cellophane; dead twigs.

1 Curve a length of wire into a random, snaky shape. Bend the wire round at the bottom to make a base.

2 Wrap stuffing around the wire along its length. Fix the stuffing to the wire with rubber bands.

3 Cut a long oval, about 16 x 8 cm, from green felt. This will be the inside of the Hydra's mouth.

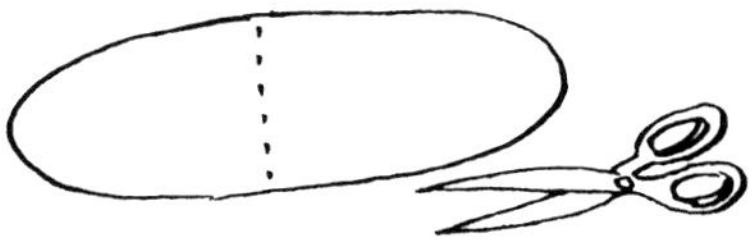

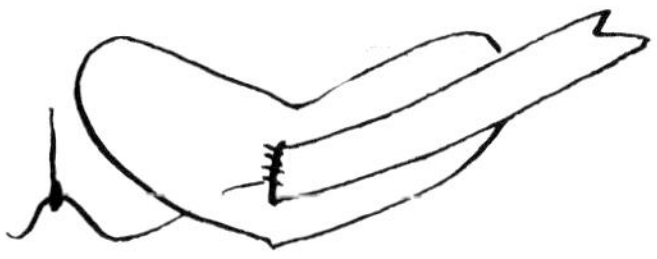

4 Cut a forked tongue from red felt and sew it or stick it inside the folded mouth.

5 Push in the foot of the stocking to make a pocket. Insert the folded mouth and sew or stick it in place.

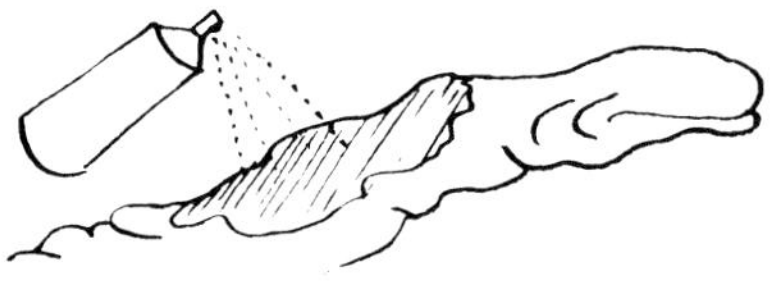

6 Slip the stocking with the head over the padded wire. Paint or spray it green. (Keep its mouth shut while you paint!)

7 Stick or sew on white felt eyes. Mark the pupils with a felt pen.

8 Make a set of Hydra heads (at least nine) and fix them to a wooden base covered in foil and blue or green cellophane to represent the watery swamp.

9 Add scenery of dead twigs and strands of green cellophane, to suggest the dead forest, poisoned by the Hydra's breath.

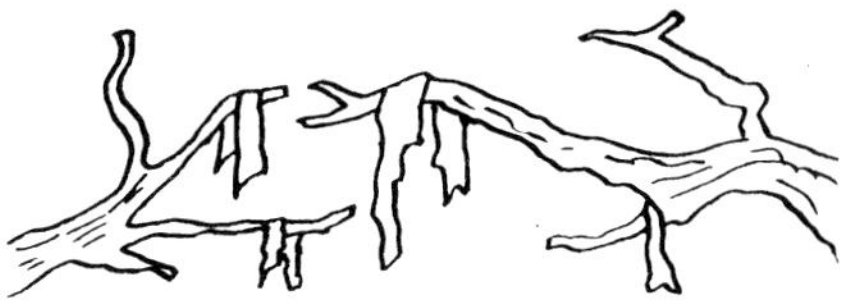

Hands-on archaeology

Name: ______________________ Date: ___________

Archaeologists studying the Roman occupation of Britain find much of their evidence underground. Some types of object survive being buried much better than others. Stone, glass and ceramics are often dug up almost unchanged; organic materials such as wood, textiles and leather usually decay, and metals may corrode or rust. Scavenging mammals and burrowing invertebrates may feed on particular materials. Fungi and bacteria break down organic substances, while water and dissolved oxygen corrode metal objects. The rate of decay is affected by the environment and by soil conditions at the burial site. Soil that is very dry and sandy, or waterlogged and peaty may slow down the processes of decay considerably.

This experiment is designed to explore the effects of burial on different objects. Record every stage on paper and with photographs. Describe the site, log the objects, predict what will happen to them, and check your predictions at the end.

Here is a suggested list of objects for your experiment. Add any more you can think of!

1 glass (a bottle or glass nugget)
2 china
3 copper coin
4 iron nail
5 scrap of lead or solder
6 thin wood (perhaps with some writing in ink on it)
7 paper
8 acorn or nut
9 cork
10 feather
11 eggshell
12 chicken bone
13 seashell
14 piece of leather
15 natural fabric, e.g. wool
16 lock of hair
17 pieces of toast (one normal and one very burnt)

Place the objects in an open box, preferably a flimsy wooden fruit box. Dig a hole in a place on the school grounds which will be undisturbed for most of the year. Fill and cover the box with soil. Make sure you mark the burial site clearly. Ideally, the box should be buried in October or November and dug up at the end of the summer term to give the processes of decay maximum time to work.

Hands-on archaeology: record sheet

Name: ____________________ Date: __________

Date of burial	Weather conditions	Soil condition
What is the site like?		
How is the deposit marked?		
Date of excavation	Weather conditions	Soil condition
What is the site like now?		

Object	Is it organic?	What do you predict will happen to it?	What did happen to it?

Cut-out signifer

Name: ____________________ Date: __________

Colour the picture of Lucius Duccius Rufinus, the **signifer**. Stick the page onto thin card and cut the figure out carefully.

XVIII

Where do they come from?

Name:____________________ Date:__________

Use the map of the Roman provinces (activity sheet V), and the information given in chapters 1 to 5 of *Minimus secundus*, to identify the characters on the right and find out their places of origin. Cut out the figures and stick them in the right places on the map. Then label the characters and their places of origin.

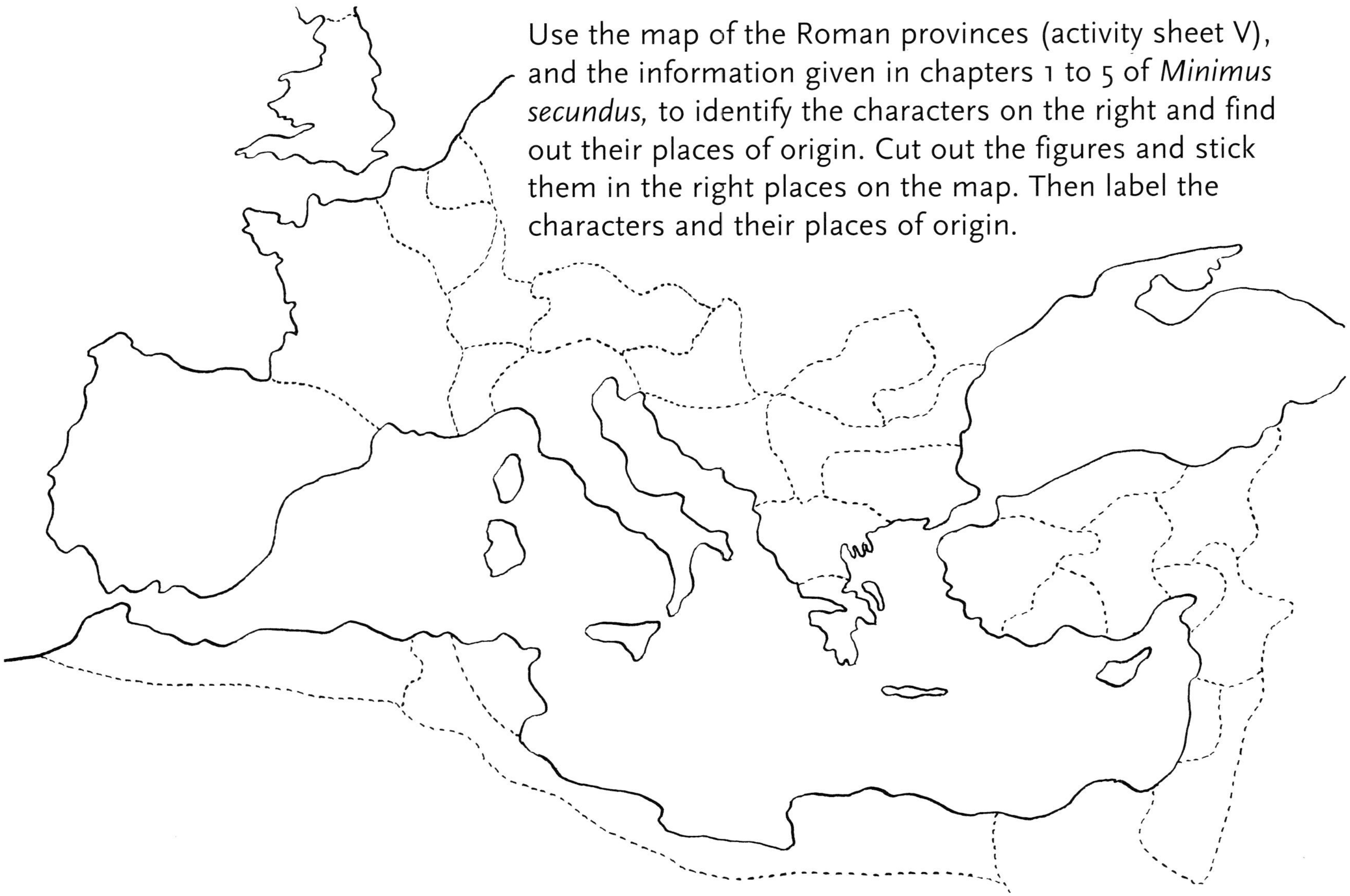

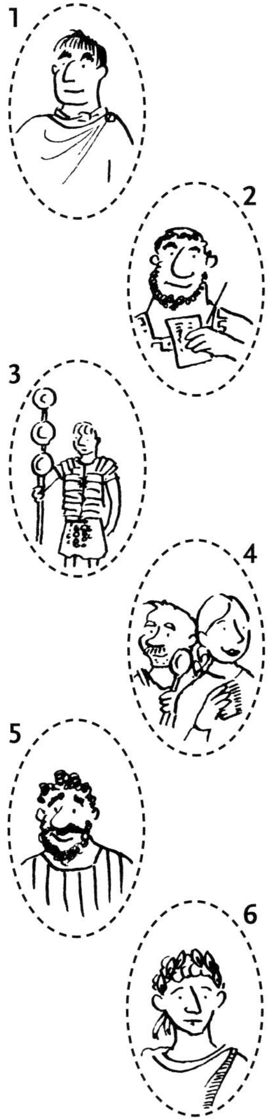

XIX

Roman bridge model

Name: ____________________ Date: __________

This bridge design is based on the Danube bridge depicted on Trajan's column. Colour in the sections of the bridge. Then stick this activity sheet onto thin card. Cut along the dotted lines. Fold the pillar interiors inwards.

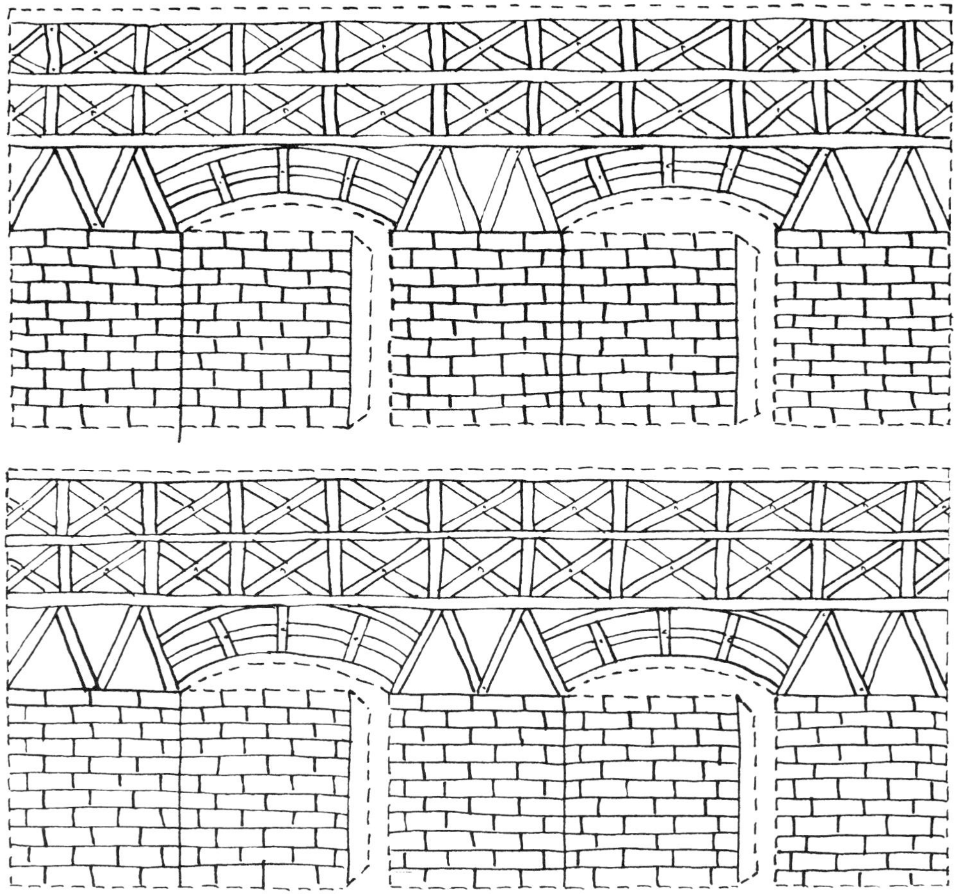

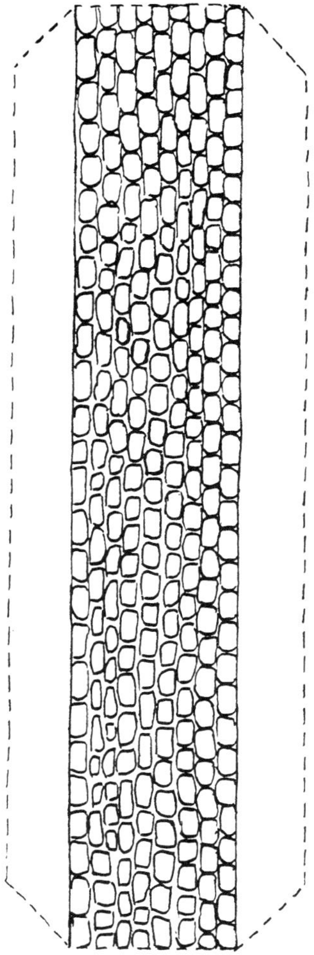

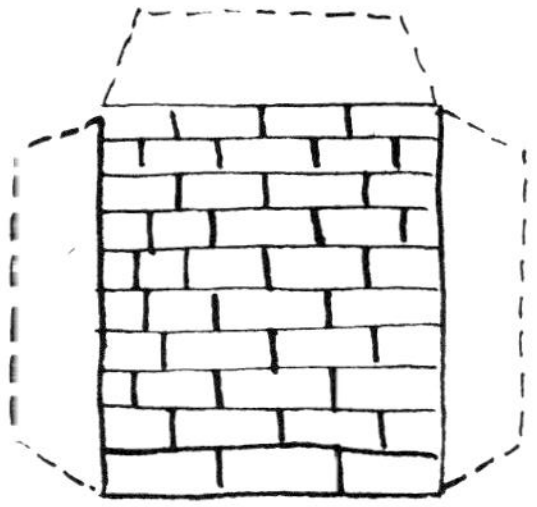

Stand the two bridge sides up, printed side outward, and stick the pillar tabs to the opposite arch.

Then stick the roadway down on top of the arches. Finally stick on the two end pieces.

Impersonal verbs

Name: ____________________ Date: ____________

These pictures illustrate some of the jobs the **signifer** had to do. Translate each sentence into English.

1 necesse est Ducciō stīpendium custōdīre.

2 facile est Ducciō signum portāre.

3 difficile est Ducciō pugnāre.

4 Ducciō placet phalerās polīre*.

5 Ducciō licet mīlitēs dūcere.

***polīre** to polish

Weather chart Name: ____________ Date: ________

Cut out the circular chart and the hanger. Fix the hanger behind the chart with a paper fastener. Cut out the triangular weather pictures and stick them to the appropriate section of the chart.

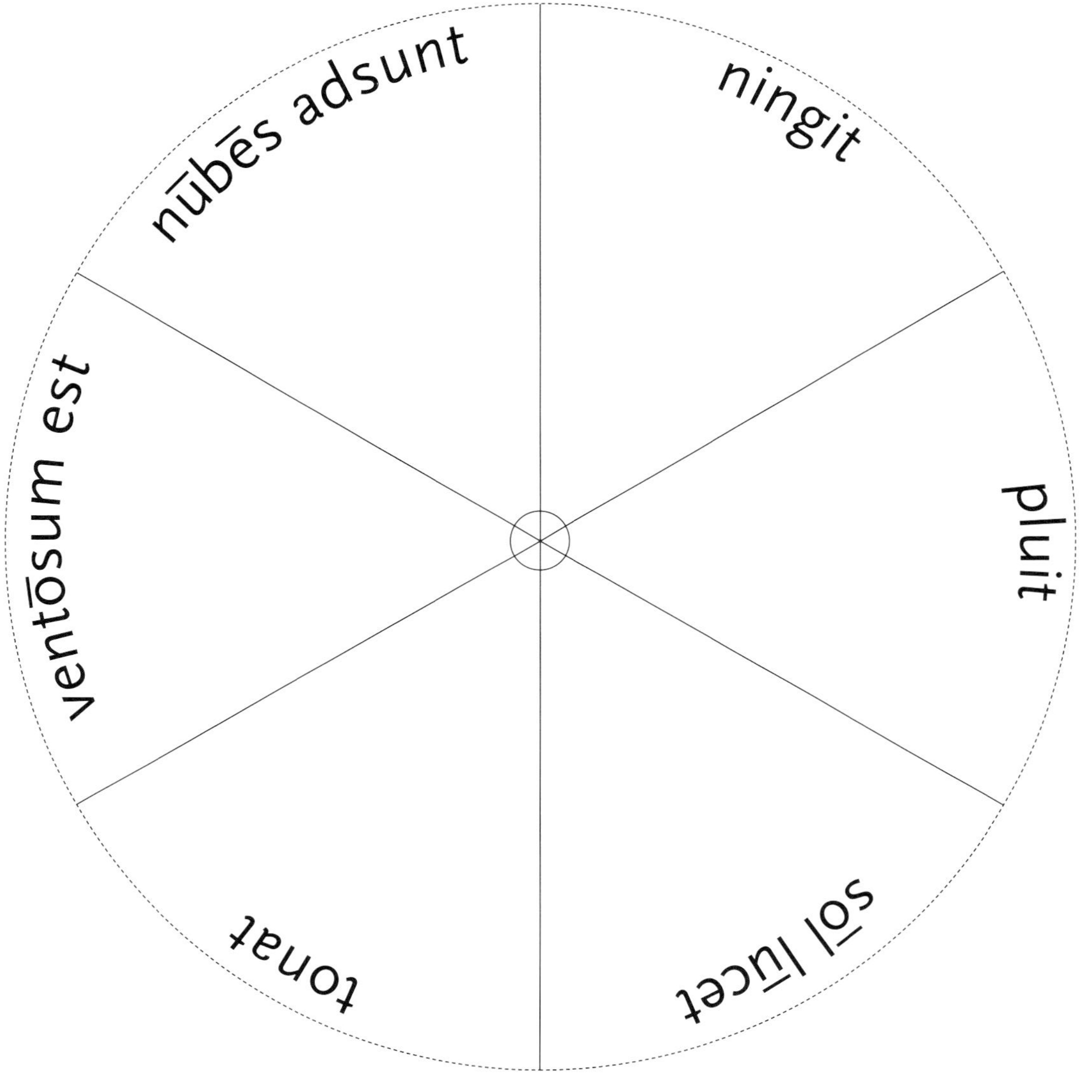

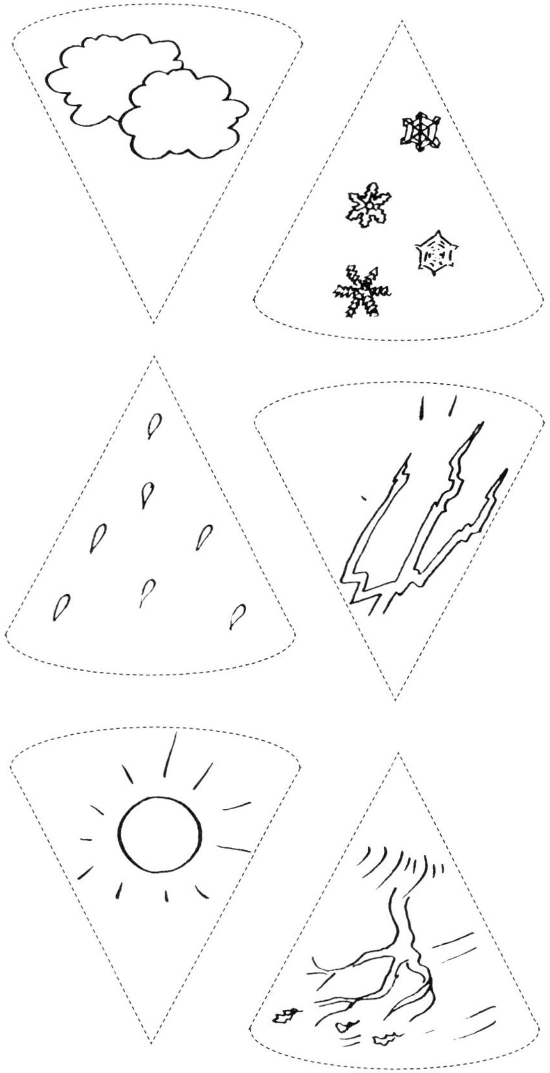

Latin abbreviations and phrases

Name: ______________________ Date: ____________

Lots of Latin abbreviations and Latin phrases are still in common use in English. Can you work out what these expressions mean?

1 a.m. ______________________________

2 p.m. ______________________________

3 etc. ______________________________

4 i.e. ______________________________

5 quid prō quō ______________________________

6 e.g. ______________________________

7 ad nauseam ______________________________

8 ad hoc ______________________________

9 sine quā nōn ______________________________

10 P.S. ______________________________

11 per sē ______________________________

12 AD ______________________________

13 NB ______________________________

14 prō tem. ______________________________

15 ad lib. ______________________________

Practice makes perfect: nouns

Name: ______________________ Date: ____________

Here are some more sentences to practise **nouns**.
Mark “v” over the verb, “s” over the subject (or subjects) and “o” over the object. Then translate each sentence into English. The first one is done for you.

S O V

Lepidīna cēnam coquit.
Lepidina is cooking the dinner.

Now you do these:

1 Candidus cibum gustat. ______________________________

____

2 Flāvius et Rūfus cibum portant. ______________________________

____

3 Corinthus pilleum gerit. ______________________________

____

4 Minimus et Vibrissa cibum cōnsūmunt. ______________________________

____

5 Rūfus cibum cōnsūmit. ______________________________

____

6 Pandōra Rūfum amat. ______________________________

____

Martial's Saturnalia poems

Name: ____________________ Date: __________

Marcus Valerius Martialis was a famous poet of the Roman Empire. We know that he was born in Spain (like the emperor Trajan) in about AD 40, and that he died before AD 105. He lived in Rome and wrote fourteen books of epigrams – short, pungent poems, often poking fun at people's conceits and bad habits. He filled two whole books with miniature poems written for the Saturnalia festival. They were intended as labels for Saturnalia presents or for food items given to party guests. Here are five of the epigrams, with translations and notes. Read them and see if you can work out how the Latin fits together. You will notice that the poems don't rhyme. The special sound of Latin poetry was created with rhythmic metre instead of the rhyme patterns which are more usual in English.

pāvōnēs mīrāris, quotiēns gemmantēs explicat ālās et potes hunc saevō trādere, dūre, coquō?	***Peacocks*** *You are amazed each time it unfolds its glittering wings – yet can you hand it over to the cruel cook, heartless man?*

Cooks like Candidus liked to roast peacocks whenever they could.

cāseus Lūnēnsis cāseus Etruscae signātus imāgine Lūnae praestābit puerīs prandia mīlle tuīs.	***Cheese from Luna*** *This cheese stamped with the emblem of Etruscan Luna will offer a thousand lunches to your slaves.*

Cheeses from the Etruscan city of Luna were huge – up to 450 kilos. Minimus would definitely approve!

canis vertragus nōn sibi, sed dominō vēnātur vertragus ācer, inlaesum leporem quī tibi dente feret.	***Hunting dog*** *The keen hunting dog hunts the hare, which he brings you undamaged by his teeth, not for himself, but for his master.*

You'll meet some more vertragi in chapter 9.

pectinēs quid faciet nūllōs hic inventūra capillōs multifidō buxus quae tibi dente datur?	***Combs*** *What shall the boxwood comb, which was given to you, do when it finds no hairs with its multiple teeth?*

Lepidina's wooden comb is in the museum at Vindolanda.

scrīnium sēlēctōs nisi dās mihī libellōs, admittam tineās trucēsque blattās.	***Bookcase*** *Unless you give me selected books, I shall let in the woodworms and the fierce cockroaches!*

Roman bookcases were boxes with lids, and compartments to keep the scrolls from being squashed.

Zodiac chart

Name: ______________________ Date: ____________

Write the name of the correct sign of the zodiac in each section of this chart. Colour the pictures and cut out the chart and the pointer. Fix the pointer to the front of the chart with a paper fastener. You can turn it round to indicate the current zodiac sign throughout the year.

Who's who?

Name: ____________________ Date: ____________

Label the characters in the picture using words from the box. Use more than one label if you need to.
(**NB** Rufus is holding the baby girl and Flavius is holding the boy!)

avia	avunculus	avus	fīlia
fīlius	frāter	geminus	īnfāns
māter	nepōs	gemina	neptis
pater	soror		

Positive and negative imperatives

Name: ______________________ Date: ____________

Choose the right command from the box below to fit into each speech bubble.

nōlī dormīre!
cavēte!
nōlī strīdere!

nōlīte pugnāre!
cāseum cōnsūme!
sedē!

intrā!
exite!
nōlī lacrimāre!

Foretelling the future

Name: ______________________ Date: ____________

In every age, people have been interested in finding out what will happen in the future. Research these four Roman and four modern forms of predicting the future and make some notes on this sheet.

Astrologer	Haruspex
Augur	Oracle

Daily horoscope	Crystal ball
Tarot cards	Palm reading

The Greek alphabet

Name: ____________________ Date: __________

Here is the Greek alphabet in both upper and lower case. We have also given you the name of each letter and the equivalent letter in English. Use the remaining space to practise writing Greek letters yourself.

Α	α	alpha	a	
Β	β	beta	b	
Γ	γ	gamma	g	
Δ	δ	delta	d	
Ε	ε	epsilon	short e	
Ζ	ζ	zeta	z	
Η	η	eta	long e	
Θ	θ	theta	th	
Ι	ι	iota	i	
Κ	κ	kappa	k	
Λ	λ	lambda	l	
Μ	μ	mu	m	
Ν	ν	nu	n	
Ξ	ξ	xi	x	
Ο	ο	omicron	short o	
Π	π	pi	p	
Ρ	ρ	rho	r	
Σ	σ, ς	sigma	s	
Τ	τ	tau	t	
Υ	υ	upsilon	y, u	
Φ	φ	phi	f	
Χ	χ	chi	kh	
Ψ	ψ	psi	ps	
Ω	ω	omega	long o	

Reading Greek letters

Name: ______________________ Date: ____________

Use the alphabet sheet XXIX to help you work out what these Greek words are in English. (Here's a clue! The first ten are all proper names.)

1	Ἡρακλης	
2	Ὀδυσσευς	
3	Περσεφωνη	
4	Ἀλεξανδερ	
5	Δημητριος	
6	Κυκλωψ	
7	Ἑλλας	
8	Ἀθηναι	
9	Παρθενων	
10	Πεγασος	
11	δραμα	
12	ἱπποποταμος	
13	ἰδεα	
14	ὀρχηστρα	
15	καταστροφη	
16	διλημμα	
17	ῥοδοδενδρον	
18	ῥινοκερος	
19	ἀσθμα	
20	πνευμονια	

The Olympian gods Name:________ Date:________

Here are the gods and goddesses of Olympus, with both their Greek and Roman names. Research their functions and special responsibilities.

Greek name in Greek	Greek name in English	Roman name in English	Functions and responsibilities
Ζευς	Zeus	Jupiter	
Ἡρα	Hera	Juno	
Ποσειδων	Poseidon	Neptune	
Ἁιδης	Hades	Pluto	
Ἀθηνη	Athene	Minerva	
Ἀπολλων	Apollo	Apollo	
Ἀρτεμις	Artemis	Diana	
Ἡφαιστος	Hephaestus	Vulcan	
Ἀφροδιτη	Aphrodite	Venus	
Ἀρης	Ares	Mars	
Δημητηρ	Demeter	Ceres	
Διονυσος	Dionysus	Bacchus	
Ἑρμης	Hermes	Mercury	

The bronze tablets

Name: ______________________ Date: ___________

The bronze votive tablets dedicated by Demetrius are difficult to read. Here is a transcription. (The translation is on page 58 of the Pupil's Book.)

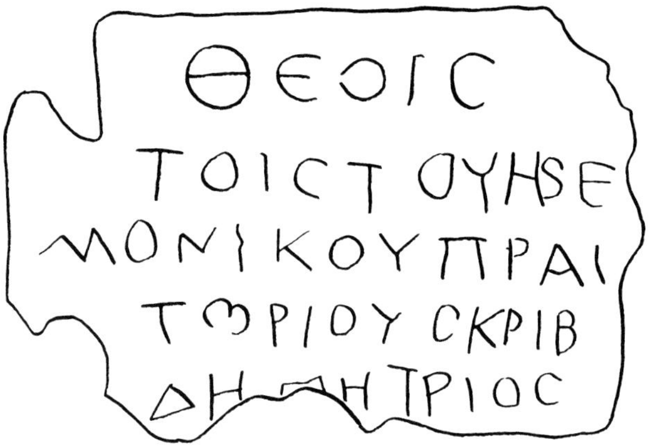

ΘΕΙΟΙΣ
ΤΟΙΣ ΤΟΥ ΗΣΕ
ΜΟΝΙΚΟΥ ΠΡΑΙ
ΤΩΡΙΟΥ ΣΚΡΙΒ
ΔΗΜΗΤΡΙΟΣ

In Greek inscriptions, the letter sigma (Σ) is often written C.

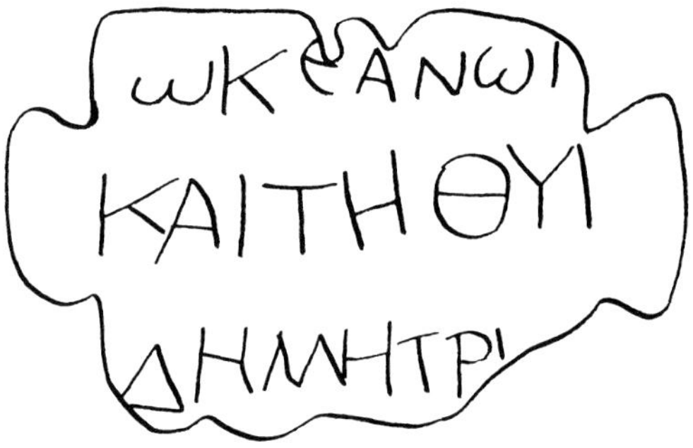

ΩΚΕΑΝΩΙ
ΚΑΙ ΤΗΘΥΙ
ΔΗΜΗΤΡΙ(ΟΣ)

Make your own votive tablet. Copy this shape onto thin card. Write a short thank-you message in pencil in large, clear letters. Then pierce the letters with a compass point or tapestry needle. Paint the finished tablet with acrylic bronze paint on both sides.

Numbers Name:______________ Date:________

Here are the numbers 1 to 10 in Latin and in five of the Romance languages which developed from Latin. Study the similarities and differences. Do some research and add the numbers in six more languages, for example German or Hindi.

	Latin	Italian	French	Spanish	Portuguese	Romanian
1	ūnus	uno	un	uno	um	un
2	duo	due	deux	dos	dois	doi
3	trēs	tre	trois	tres	três	trei
4	quattuor	quattro	quatre	cuatro	quarto	patru
5	quīnque	cinque	cinq	cinco	cinco	cinci
6	sex	sei	six	seis	seis	sase
7	septem	sette	sept	siete	sete	sapte
8	octō	otto	huit	ocho	oito	opt
9	novem	nove	neuf	nueve	nove	noua
10	decem	dieci	dix	diez	dez	zece
1						
2						
3						
4						
5						
6						
7						
8						
9						
10						

Number matching game

Name: ____________________ Date: __________

Cut out and shuffle the number cards. Then try to match each figure with the correct Latin number word.

I	ŪNUS	VI	SEX
II	DUO	VII	SEPTEM
III	TRĒS	VIII	OCTŌ
IV	QUATTUOR	IX	NOVEM
V	QUĪNQUE	X	DECEM

Cardinal and ordinal numbers

Name: ____________________ Date: __________

How many English words can you find that are derived from the Latin cardinal and ordinal numbers?

Cardinal numbers

1 ūnus/a/um
2 duo/duae/duo
3 trēs/trēs/tria
4 quattuor
5 quīnque
6 sex
7 septem
8 octō
9 novem
10 decem

Ordinal numbers

1st prīmus/a/um
2nd secundus/a/um
3rd tertius/a/um
4th quartus/a/um
5th quīntus/a/um
6th sextus/a/um
7th septimus/a/um
8th octāvus/a/um
9th novus/a/um
10th decimus/a/um

Animal snap

Name: ____________________ Date: __________

rāna	blatta	lacerta	elephantus	echīnus	sciūrus
rāna	blatta	lacerta	elephantus	echīnus	sciūrus
vacca	talpa	gallīna	taurus	equus	ursus
vacca	talpa	gallīna	taurus	equus	ursus
vespa	bālaena	sīmia	cunīculus	grīllus	lupus
vespa	bālaena	sīmia	cunīculus	grīllus	lupus

Slave placards

Name: ____________________ Date: __________

Study the four slaves in these pictures and write an appropriate placard for each one. You should mention the slave's age, their origin, the language or languages they can speak, their skills and their physical condition. The slaves should not be given names. When you have finished labelling the slaves, discuss the relative prices of the four. What kind of job might each one be given?

Past participle derivations

Name: ______________________ Date: ____________

These four past participles form the basis of a large number of English words. Use a dictionary to find as many derivations as you can.

scrīptus	ductus
missus	**positus**

The judgement of Paris

Name: ____________________ Date: __________

The three goddesses, Hera, Athene and Aphrodite, all offered Paris bribes to persuade him to choose them as the most beautiful. Write your own version of the goddesses' tempting offers to Paris.

Roman measurements

Name: ____________________ Date: __________

The Romans measured length in **ūnciae**, **pedēs**, **passūs** and **mīlia passuum** – inches, feet, paces and miles. There were 12 inches in one foot. (The Roman foot was a tiny bit shorter than a British foot but a British ruler will do perfectly well for measuring.) There were 5 feet in a pace and 1,000 paces in a mile.

Try these measuring and maths exercises:

- Find a ruler that is marked in inches. Measure and record the length of different objects in the classroom, for example your desk, a *Minimus* book, your arm.

- A pace is supposed to be a step taken at full stretch. Are your paces equal to five times your foot measurement?

- Measure some larger objects (e.g. your classroom, the playground) in feet and in paces.

XLI The groma

Name: ____________________ Date: __________

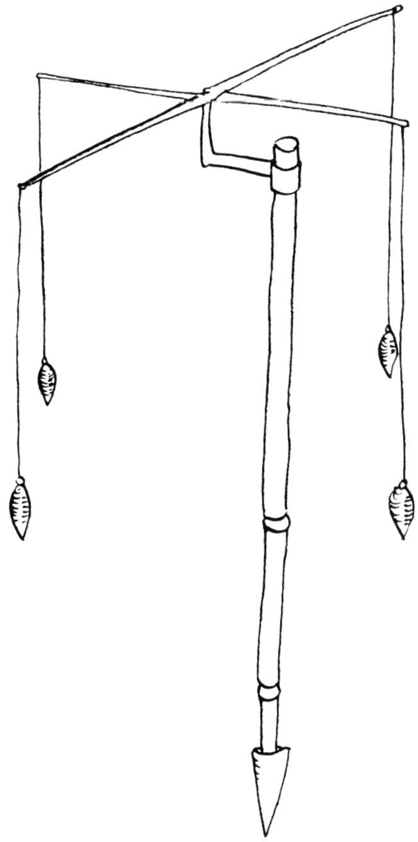

The groma was the Roman equivalent of the modern surveyor's theodolite. It was used to establish straight lines and right angles. The groma consisted of a straight shaft with a spike on the end for fixing it into the ground, a rotating bracket and two arms crossed at right angles, with lead weights suspended at the ends of the arms to make sure that the groma was perfectly vertical. The surveyor sighted along the arms of the groma to mark out a straight line on the ground.

To make a simplified working model of a groma, you will need:

- a straight wooden shaft (e.g. a broomstick) with a sharpened end
- two equal-sized pieces of wood
- four lengths of string
- four weights (e.g. lead curtain weights or steel washers)

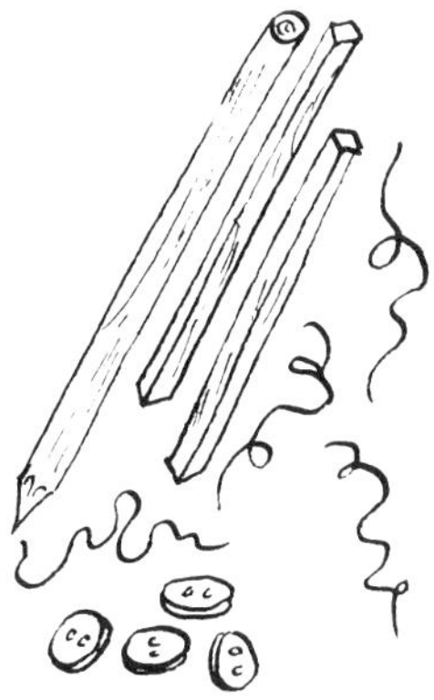

Join the two shorter pieces of wood at right angles, preferably with a lap-joint. Fasten the cross piece to the broomstick with a large nail, drilling a hole first to prevent splitting.

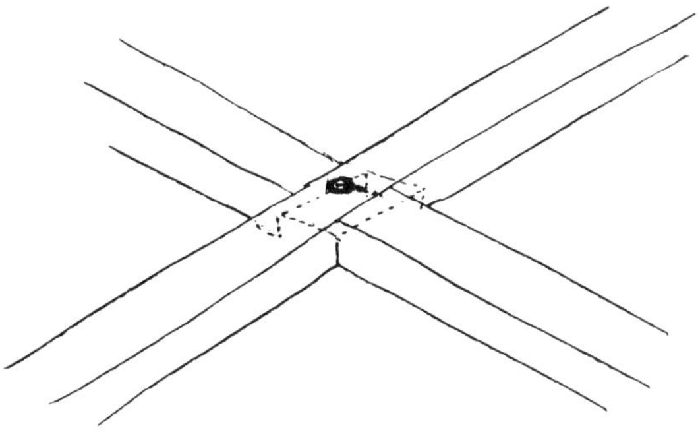

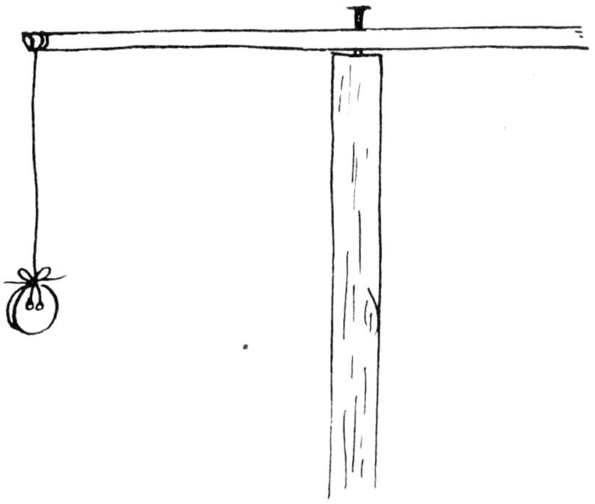

Tie the strings to the ends of the arms and suspend the weights from them, making sure that all the strings are the same length.

Plan of a Roman fortress

Name: ______________________ Date: ___________

Most Roman military fortresses were built with the same basic layout and orientation. This plan shows the typical elements of a Roman fortress. Use library resources and the internet to find out about the different buildings and their uses. Match the numbers to the correct labels.

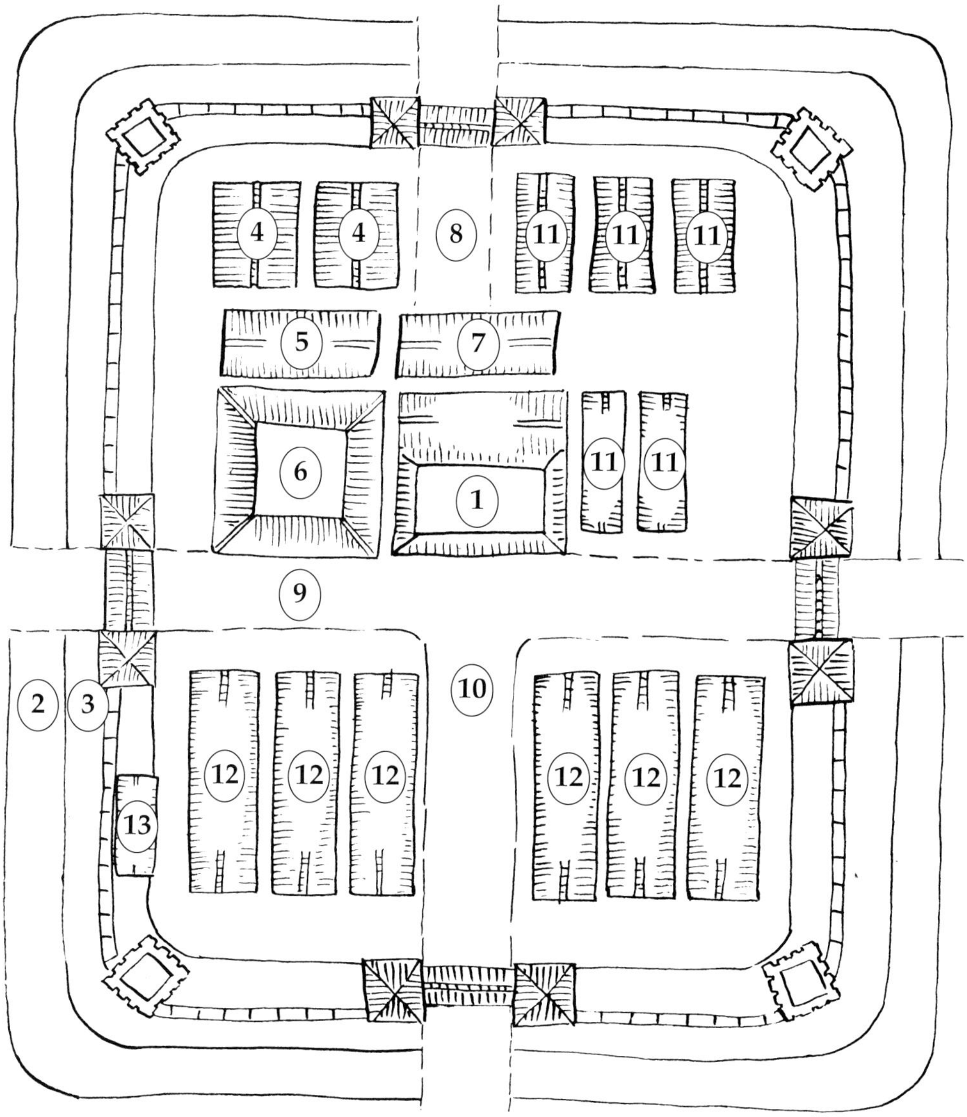

latrīna
vallum
horrea
officīna
balnea
via Prīncipālis
valētūdinārium
contubernia
via Decumāna
praetōrium
prīncipia
via Praetōria
fossa

Minimus and Minima

Name: ______________________ Date: ____________

Translate the captions and draw the cartoons in the boxes!

1

ecce Minimus!

____

2

ecce Minima!

____

3

Minimus Minimam spectat.

____

4

Minima ērubēscit.*

____

5

Minima Minimum spectat.

____

6

Minima cāseum portat.

____

7

cāseum Minima omittit!

____

8

Minimus Minimam adiuvat.

____

9

Minimus et Minima
cāseum cōnsūmunt.

____

*__ērubēscit__ blushes

Make Pandora's fan

Name: ______________________ Date: ___________

You will need: 2 sheets of A3 paper (or a strip of paper approximately 90 x 15 cm), masking tape, glue, two flat wooden or stiff cardboard handles.

Cut the paper in half lengthwise to make long, narrow strips.

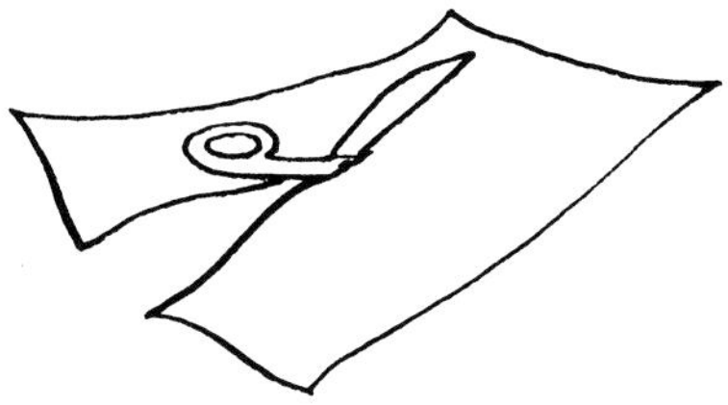

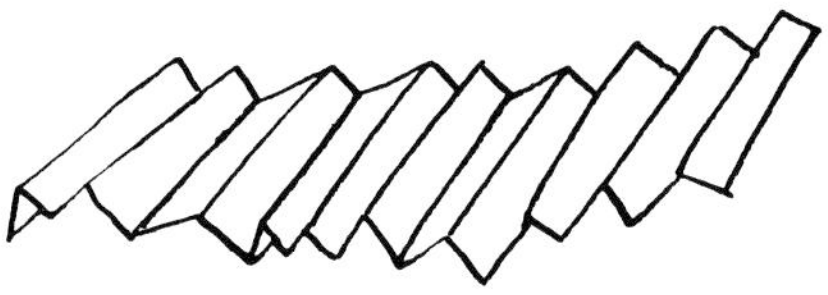

Mark the long edge of the paper at 2 cm intervals. Very carefully, fold the paper into 2 cm wide concertina pleats. It is important that the folds are straight and parallel.

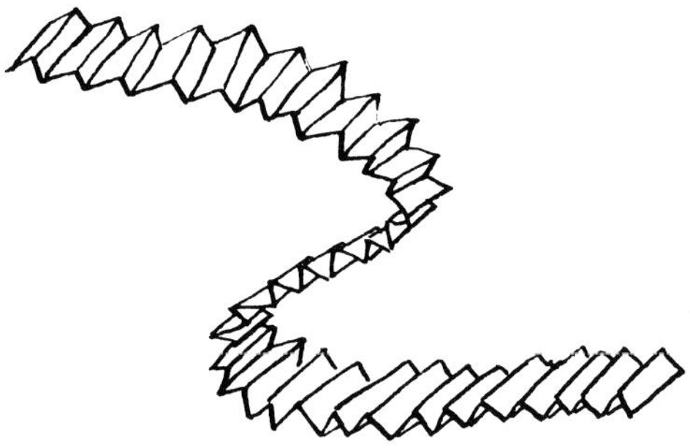

You will need three pleated strips. Stick them together with masking tape into one long strip.

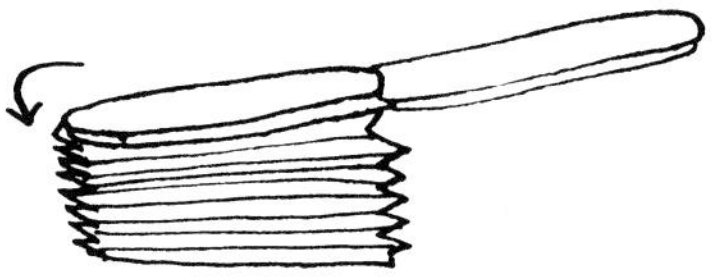

The handles should be about 25–30 cm long. Make them from stiff card or from wood the thickness of a ruler, or from lolly sticks stuck together by overlapping their ends. Stick one handle to each end of the long pleated strip of paper.

Squeeze the handles together at the top, compressing the pleats. You need to glue and tape the top edge of the paper fan to keep the pleats from unfolding.

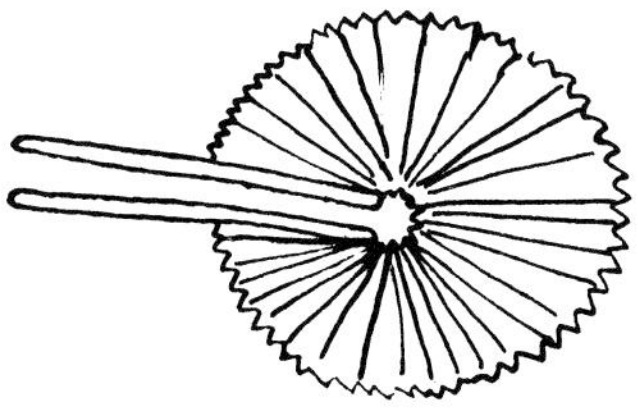

When the glue is dry, unfold the handles to open up the fan.

Centaurs

Name: ______________________ Date: ____________

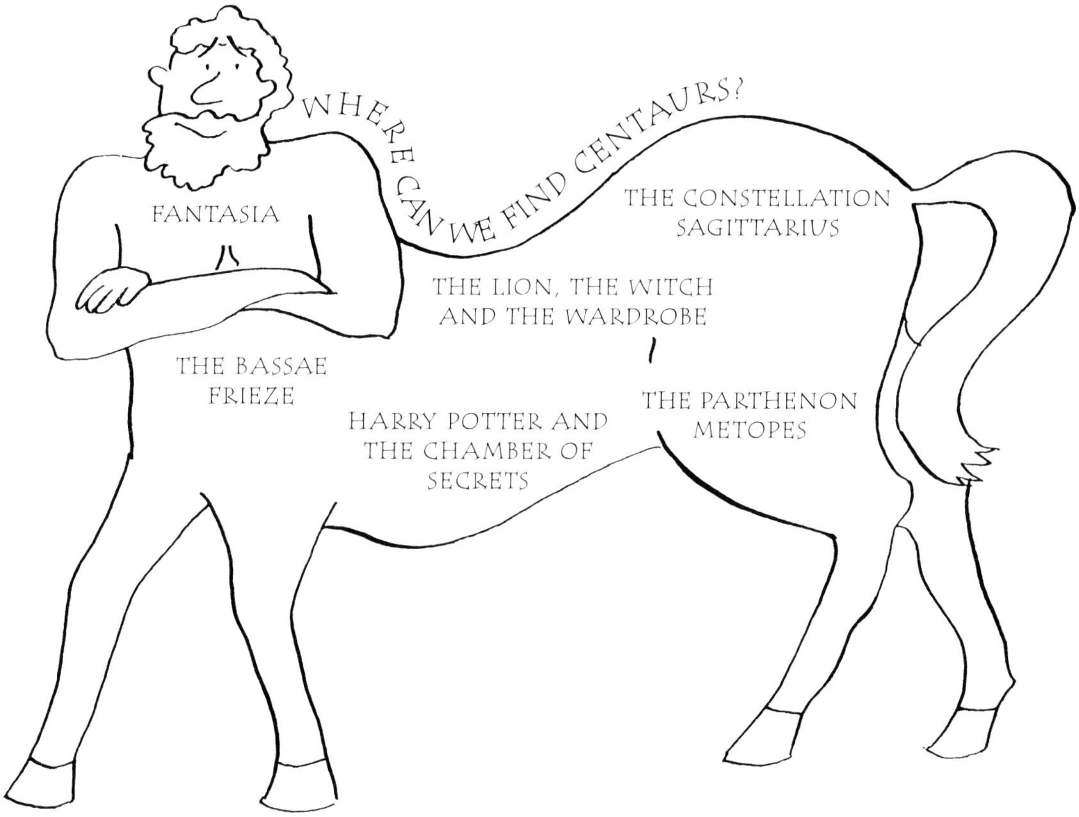

Write an acrostic poem about a centaur.

C ____

E ____

N ____

T ____

A ____

U ____

R ____

The transformations of Thetis

Name: ______________________ Date: ____________

In the story of Peleus and Thetis, the sea-goddess undergoes a series of transformations in her attempts to evade Peleus's clutches. She turns herself into fire, water, a lion and a serpent, and finally a giant cuttlefish.
The drawing shows this scene depicted on a Greek vase.

- Consider the contest between Peleus and his unwilling bride. How might he have felt, trying to hold her through her changes? How might he have kept hold of her? Write a poem, with alternate verses spoken by Thetis and Peleus, to describe the struggle.
- Write a story about someone with shape-shifting powers.
- Research myths and folk tales with the theme of transformation.

Words to remember

Chapter 1

Nouns

equus (m) horse

mīlitēs (m pl) soldiers

pompa (f) parade

Verbs

appropinquat he approaches/is approaching

audit he hears/is hearing

vocat he calls/is calling

Adjectives

laetus happy

optimus excellent/the best

Adverbs

subitō suddenly

tum then

Exclamations

ecce! look!

ēheu! oh no!

euge! hooray!

Idioms

aliī . . . aliī . . . some . . . others . . .

ita vērō yes

Chapter 2

Nouns

arma (n pl) weapons

bellum (n) war

cēna (f) dinner

dea (f) goddess

imperātor (m) emperor

legiōnēs (f pl) legions

mare (n) sea

Verbs

aedificō I build

habeō I have

superō I win

Question words

cūr? why?

quid? what?

quis? who?

ubi? where?

Conjunctions

quod because

sed but

Adverbs

nunc now

semper always

Chapter 3

Noun

via (f) road

Verbs

sedet she sits

Impersonal verbs

advesperāscit it is becoming dark

difficile est it is difficult

necesse est it is necessary/must

pluit it is raining

tonat it is thundering

Adverbs

celeriter quickly

cotīdiē every day

iterum again

lentē slowly

tandem at last

Chapter 4

Nouns

amīcus (m) friend

amphorae (f pl) jars

flūmen (n) river

frūmentum (n) grain

nāvēs (f pl) ships

Verbs

facile est it is easy

labōrāre to work

Adjectives

malus/a/um bad

maximus/a/um very big

Chapter 5

Noun

iuvenis (m) young man

Adverb

tamen however

Verbs

erat he was

intrat he enters

reveniunt they return

Infinitives

facere to make/to do

invenīre to find

Chapter 6

Nouns

cibus (m) food

dōnum (n) present

lectus (m) couch

liber (m) book

Verbs

facit it makes

fundit he pours

lacrimat he cries

revenit she returns

Adverb

hodiē today

Adjective

pulcher/pulchra/pulchrum beautiful

Chapter 7

Nouns

cubiculum (n) bedroom

fīlia (f) daughter

fīlius (m) son

terra (f) earth, land, ground

Adjective

fortis/fortis/forte brave

Preposition

sub under

Verbs (given in the ***infinitive*** form here)

accipere to receive

adiuvāre to help

advenīre to arrive

pōnere to put

revenīre to return

Chapter 8

Nouns

annus (m) year

nauta (m) sailor

nāvis (f) ship

Verbs

grātiās agere to thank

habitāre to live

legere to read

nāvigāre to sail

scrībere to write

sedēre to sit

vidēre to see

Adjectives

fessus/a/um tired

tūtus/a/um safe

Chapter 9

Nouns

diēs (m) day

gladius (m) sword

nōmen (n) name

vīlla (f) house

Verbs

abesse to be absent

adesse to be present

amāre to love/to like

dare to give

esse to be

petere to seek/make for

portāre to carry

posse to be able

venīre to come

Adverbs

fortasse perhaps

ōlim once upon a time (past) *or* at some time (future)

postrīdiē on the next day

Chapter 10

Noun

vīta (f) life

Verbs

ēmere to buy

festīnāre to hurry

Participles

missus sent

positus positioned

trāditus handed over

vīnctus tied up

Adjectives

melior/melior/melius better

novus/a/um new

sōlus/a/um alone/lonely

Chapter 11

Nouns

porta (f) gate

prīncipia (n pl) headquarters

Verbs

aedificāre to build

bibere to drink

habēre to have

īnspicere to inspect

servāre to save

stāre to stand

Adjectives

invītus/a/um unwilling

parvus/a/um small

vīvus/a/um alive

Chapter 12

Nouns

ānulus (m) ring

līberta (f) freedwoman

uxor (f) wife

Verb

trādere to hand over

Adverb

intereā meanwhile

Idiom

mēcum with me

RISING STARS
ASSESSMENT

SCIENCE
UNIT TESTS

YEAR
6

Louise Moore
Revised by: Steve Sizmur
Series Editor: Colin McCarty

RISING STARS

Rising Stars UK Ltd, 7 Hatchers Mews, Bermondsey Street, London SE1 3GS

www.risingstars-uk.com

All facts are correct at time of going to press.

Published 2006
Second edition 2006
Third edition 2007
This edition 2008
Reprinted 2009 (twice), 2010, 2011 (3 times)

Editorial: Denise Moulton
Design: Oxford Designers & Illustrators and Clive Sutherland
Illustrations: Oxford Designers & Illustrators
Cover design: Burville-Riley Partnership

Rising Stars is grateful to the following people who contributed to the development of these materials:

Language accessibility consultant: Vivien Kilburn
Research statistician: Tony Kiek

We are grateful to the following schools for helping us to develop this edition:

Sandra Barry, St Edmund Campion Catholic Primary School, Maidenhead, Berkshire;
Sarah Blunt, Brooklands Primary School, Romney Marsh, Kent;
Linda Cullen, Newington Community School, Ramsgate, Kent;
Simon Cuming, Whitehills Primary School, Northampton;
Catherine Edwards, Park Mead Primary School, Cranleigh, Surrey;
Helen Fitch, Dunton Green Primary School, Sevenoaks, Kent;
Dawn McKenna, Cuerden Church School, Bamber Bridge, Lancashire;
Anita Mutton and Mary Cronin, St Mary's Church of England Primary School, Banbury, Oxfordshire;
Criag Robertson, Chellaston Junior School, Derby;
Steve Sutherland, Harwell Primary School, Harwell Didcot, Oxfordshire;
Kate Towsey, Park Way Primary School, Maidstone, Kent.

British Library Cataloguing in Publication Data.
A CIP record for this book is available from the British Library.

ISBN: 978 1 84680 397 0

Printed by Ashford Colour Press Ltd

MIX
Paper from responsible sources
FSC® C011748

Contents

Quick start guide to Rising Stars Assessment

Step 1 Introduce the tests

The tests are based on the content of the units of the QCA Scheme of Work for Science. Explain to the class that they will take up to four unit tests each year. The four unit tests are each worth ten marks and can be used as follows:

- Test 1 – to assess prior learning of the topic;
- Test 2 – to assess knowledge and understanding after teaching the topic;
- Test 3 – to assess scientific enquiry skills after teaching the topic;
- Test 4 – for end-of-year assessment.

This will give pupils the opportunity to show what they know and can do. The tests are designed to check understanding and results can be used to record and monitor progress throughout the year.

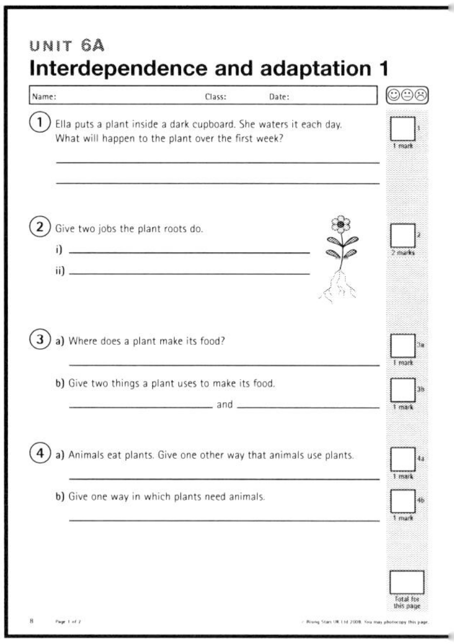
UNIT 6A
Interdependence and adaptation 1

Name: Class: Date:

1 Ella puts a plant inside a dark cupboard. She waters it each day. What will happen to the plant over the first week? (1 mark)

2 Give two jobs the plant roots do.
i)
ii) (2 marks)

3 a) Where does a plant make its food? (1 mark)
b) Give two things a plant uses to make its food. ___ and ___ (1 mark)

4 a) Animals eat plants. Give one other way that animals use plants. (1 mark)
b) Give one way in which plants need animals. (1 mark)

Total for this page

Step 2 Mark the test

Use the mark scheme and your own professional judgement to award marks. Do not award half marks. The tests can be swapped and marked by pupils – this is a good opportunity for peer assessment.

The mark schemes include details of the National Curriculum level of each question.

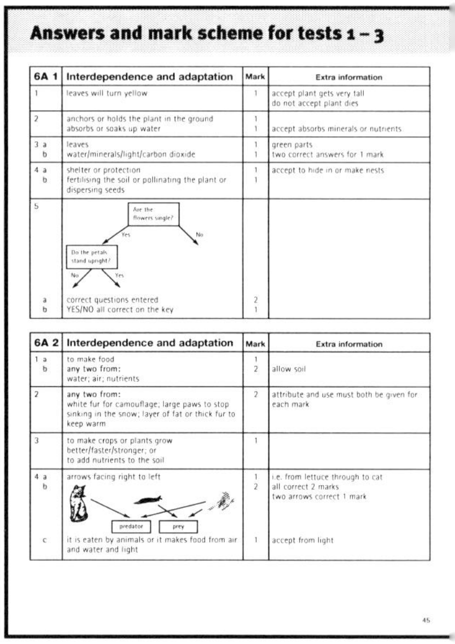
Answers and mark scheme for tests 1 – 3

6A 1	Interdependence and adaptation	Mark	Extra information
1	leaves will turn yellow	1	accept plant gets very tall do not accept plant dies
2	anchors or holds the plant in the ground absorbs or soaks up water	1 1	 accept absorbs minerals or nutrients
3 a b	leaves water/minerals/light/carbon dioxide	1 1	green parts two correct answers for 1 mark
4 a b	shelter or protection fertilising the soil or pollinating the plant or dispersing seeds	1 1	accept to hide in or make nests
5 a b	Are the flowers single? Yes / No; Do the petals stand upright? No / Yes correct questions entered YES/NO all correct on the key	 2 1	

6A 2	Interdependence and adaptation	Mark	Extra information
1 a b	to make food any two from: water; air; nutrients	1 2	 allow soil
2	any two from: white fur for camouflage; large paws to stop sinking in the snow; layer of fat or thick fur to keep warm	2	attribute and use must both be given for each mark
3	to make crops or plants grow better/faster/stronger; or to add nutrients to the soil	1	
4 a b c	arrows facing right to left predator / prey it is eaten by animals or it makes food from air and water and light	1 2 1	i.e. from lettuce through to cat all correct 2 marks two arrows correct 1 mark accept from light

45

Step 3 Generate a level

Use the mark and level threshold tables to convert the pupil's mark to a sub-level. The final row in each table gives an overall sub-level for each term's end-of-unit tests. If you have the CD-ROM version of *Science Unit Tests*, you can use the interactive Level Calculator to convert marks to levels automatically.

The mark and level threshold pages also include a summary of the distribution of marks and levels for each test.

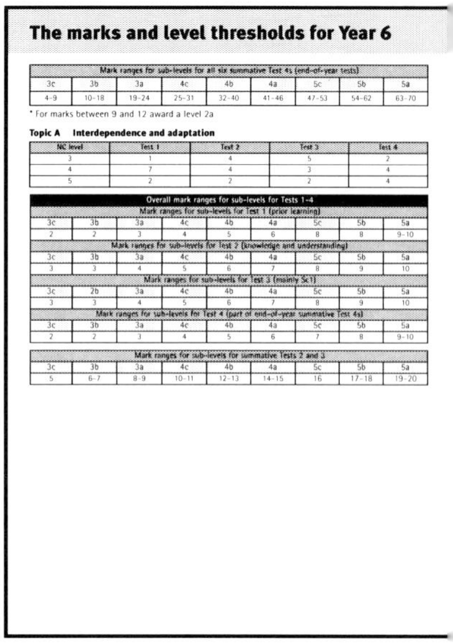
The marks and level thresholds for Year 6

Mark ranges for sub-levels for all six summative Test 4s (end-of-year tests)								
3c	3b	3a	4c	4b	4a	5c	5b	5a
4–9	10–18	19–24	25–31	32–40	41–46	47–53	54–62	63–70

* For marks between 9 and 12 award a level 2a

Topic A Interdependence and adaptation

NC level	Test 1	Test 2	Test 3	Test 4
3	1	4	5	2
4	7	4	3	4
5	2	2	2	4

Overall mark ranges for sub-levels for Tests 1-4								
Mark ranges for sub-levels for Test 1 (prior learning)								
3c	3b	3a	4c	4b	4a	5c	5b	5a
2	2	3	4	5	6	8	8	9–10
Mark ranges for sub-levels for Test 2 (knowledge and understanding)								
3c	3b	3a	4c	4b	4a	5c	5b	5a
3	3	4	5	6	7	8	9	10
Mark ranges for sub-levels for Test 3 (mainly Sc1)								
3c	2b	3a	4c	4b	4a	5c	5b	5a
3	3	4	5	6	7	8	9	10
Mark ranges for sub-levels for Test 4 (part of end-of-year summative Test 4s)								
3c	3b	3a	4c	4b	4a	5c	5b	5a
2	2	3	4	5	6	7	8	9–10

Mark ranges for sub-levels for summative Tests 2 and 3								
3c	3b	3a	4c	4b	4a	5c	5b	5a
5	6–7	8–9	10–11	12–13	14–15	16	17–18	19–20

Step 4 Feed back to the pupils

Use a five-minute session with pupils to talk through the test and give them the opportunity to make their own corrections. Identify strengths and weaknesses and agree targets for learning.

Encourage pupils to complete the pupil record sheets for each unit after each test. Pupils can keep these sheets and use them to record their progress throughout the year.

Introduction

Why use Rising Stars Assessment?

Rising Stars *Science Unit Tests* have been developed to help teachers provide effective assessment for learning in science and to deliver formative assessment of progress across Years 1 to 6. The tests are organised by units, to reflect the structure of the QCA Scheme of Work for Science, and have been:

- designed by an assessment expert;
- written by primary science assessment specialists;
- checked by practising classroom teachers;
- reviewed by a language expert to ensure accessibility of the language;
- trialled with schools;
- equated and standardised by an assessment expert to ensure reliability of the levels.

The tests are easy to use and mark. The scores for each test have been converted to sub-levels. The sub-levels can then be used to investigate, monitor and report on the performance of every pupil by:

- plotting each pupil's progress from term to term (summative assessment);
- diagnosing each pupil's strengths and weaknesses in each topic of the QCA Scheme of Work for Science (diagnostic assessment);
- informing your own assessment for learning strategy and supporting your lesson planning (formative assessment).

Combined, the results from the tests can be used to gather reliable evidence to assist target setting and predict a pupil's future performance.

A National Curriculum level is given to each question in every test. The table below summarises the range of levels covered in each year. Further detail is provided on the mark schemes, the pupil record sheets and the mark and level threshold section.

Year 1	Year 2	Year 3	Year 4	Year 5	Year 6
1c–2b	1c–3a	2c–4b	2c–4a	3c–5c	3c–5a

About the *Science Unit Tests*

The tests are designed to assess knowledge, understanding and skills taught through the units of the QCA Scheme of Work for Science. The tests for each unit are structured as follows:

- Test 1 – to assess prior learning;
- Tests 2 and 3 – to assess knowledge and understanding after teaching the unit. Test 2 focuses on knowledge and understanding while Test 3 focuses on assessing scientific enquiry skills (Sc1);
- Test 4 – for end-of-year summative assessment.

Each test is worth ten marks. Further information about these tests is provided in the section How to use *Science Unit Tests*.

Determining prior learning

Test 1 is designed for use before teaching a unit in KS2 so that the teacher is able to determine the prior knowledge and understanding of individuals and the class as a whole. The lessons that follow may then be focused on the areas the pupils have yet to learn. Much empirical and anecdotal evidence indicates that the time spent investigating prior learning is recovered through reducing the amount of time wasted on areas that are already understood.

Measuring summative and diagnostic progress for a topic

At the end of each unit, Tests 2 and 3 may be used to:

- measure the 'value added' through the teaching of the topic;
- determine the pupils' progress and their sub-levels;
- explore where further teaching may be required;
- assist with target setting.

Summative assessment for the year

If your school's assessment policy values an overall test toward the end of the academic year, it is recommended that all six Test 4s be used in order to obtain a summative level for the year. (If only five topics have been covered, you may scale the marks to obtain a level.) We suggest they be given in two sessions to prevent pupil fatigue.

How to use *Science Unit Tests*

Preparation and timings

1 Copy the required number of sheets to form the chosen assessment.

2 Ensure pupils are seated appropriately to prevent overlooking each other's papers.

3 Pupils will need pens or pencils, rulers and erasers. Angle measurers should be available. Pupils should be encouraged to cross out answers rather than rub them out.

4 There are no time limits for the tests, but a pair (e.g. Tests 2 and 3) should take about 15-20 minutes. Help with reading may be given using the same rules as when providing a reader with QCA KS2 tests (i.e. 25% extra time allowance for poor readers).

Supporting pupils during the tests

Before the test, explain to the pupils that the test is an opportunity to show what they know, understand and can do. They will not be asked questions about topics they have not yet been taught.

Many pupils will be able to work independently in the tests, with minimal support from the person administering the tests (usually the teacher or teaching assistant). This person may encourage the pupils to 'have a go' at a question, or to move on to a fresh question if they appear to be stuck, ensuring that no pupil becomes distressed.

It is important that pupils receive appropriate support, but are not unfairly advantaged or disadvantaged. Throughout the tests, therefore, the teacher may read, explain or sign to a pupil any parts of the test that include instructions, for example, by demonstrating how to circle an answer.

With younger age groups you may also consider projecting the test onto a whiteboard to support a whole class or group to take the end-of-unit tests. You may choose to refer to the words on the whiteboard and read them aloud so that pupils can follow them on the screen and on their own test paper. They can then write their answers on their papers individually.

Marking the test

Use the detailed mark scheme and your professional judgement to award marks. Do not award half marks. Note that a number of questions in each test may require pupils to do more than one thing for one mark. This reflects the style of the optional and end of Key Stage tests. Questions of this nature have been included to familiarise pupils with the types of questions they will encounter in those tests.

Pupils should be encouraged to make their own corrections. In this way they will become more aware of their own strengths and weaknesses.

Use a five-minute feedback session with a pupil to help them review and transfer the information to the pupil record sheets. This provides a useful opportunity to discuss progress and to explore any areas of uncertainty.

Obtaining levels and sub-levels

The mark and level thresholds (pages 63–66) give the mark ranges for each sub-level for each test. The final row in each table gives an overall mark range of each sub-level for the Test 4s, which may act as the summative record of progress in each topic.

The CD-ROM version of *Science Unit Tests* includes an interactive Level Calculator, which allows you to enter the raw score gained on each test by each pupil. The sub-levels are displayed including:

- a sub-level for each test;
- a level for the unit from the combined Tests 2 and 3;
- an overall year level for the Test 4s.

The CD-ROM also includes a data exporter to allow you to export data from the Level Calculator. This enables you to manipulate test information easily and allows for analysis of the data by pupil, by group and by class.

Completing the pupil record sheets

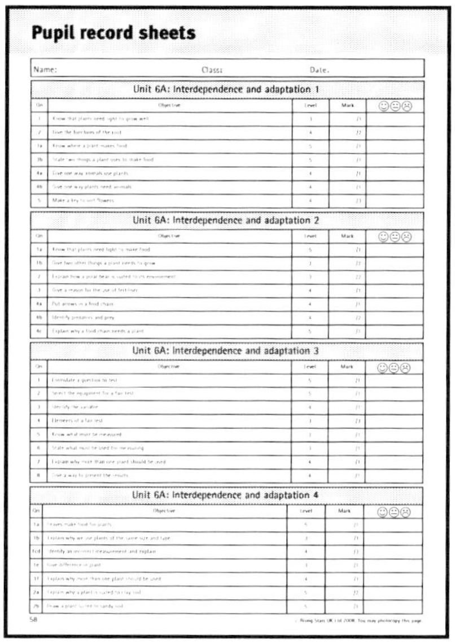
Pupil record sheets

Name: Class: Date:

Unit 6A: Interdependence and adaptation 1

Unit 6A: Interdependence and adaptation 2

Unit 6A: Interdependence and adaptation 3

Unit 6A: Interdependence and adaptation 4

These objective sheets refer to the detailed learning objectives for primary science for each question in the four topic tests. The National Curriculum level of each mark is also given so that pupils may see at which levels they are gaining marks. It provides evidence of what pupils should be concentrating on to improve their performance. Teachers have also indicated that this detailed information is extremely useful to inform lesson planning and support assessment for learning strategies.

This way of working uses assessment in an open way. It helps each pupil to identify his or her strengths and weaknesses. Pupils can then use this information to help them in their future learning.

UNIT 6A
Interdependence and adaptation 1

Name: Class: Date:

☺ 😐 ☹

1 Ella puts a plant inside a dark cupboard. She waters it each day. What will happen to the plant over the first week?

____

____

1 | 1 mark

2 Give two jobs the plant roots do.

i) ______________________________

ii) ______________________________

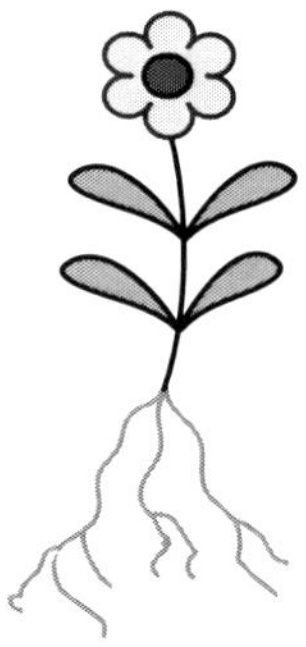

2 | 2 marks

3 a) Where does a plant make its food?

____

3a | 1 mark

b) Give two things a plant uses to make its food.

______________ and ______________

3b | 1 mark

4 a) Animals eat plants. Give one other way that animals use plants.

____

4a | 1 mark

b) Give one way in which plants need animals.

____

4b | 1 mark

Total for this page

UNIT 6A

Interdependence and adaptation 1

5 The key is used to sort the flowering plants.

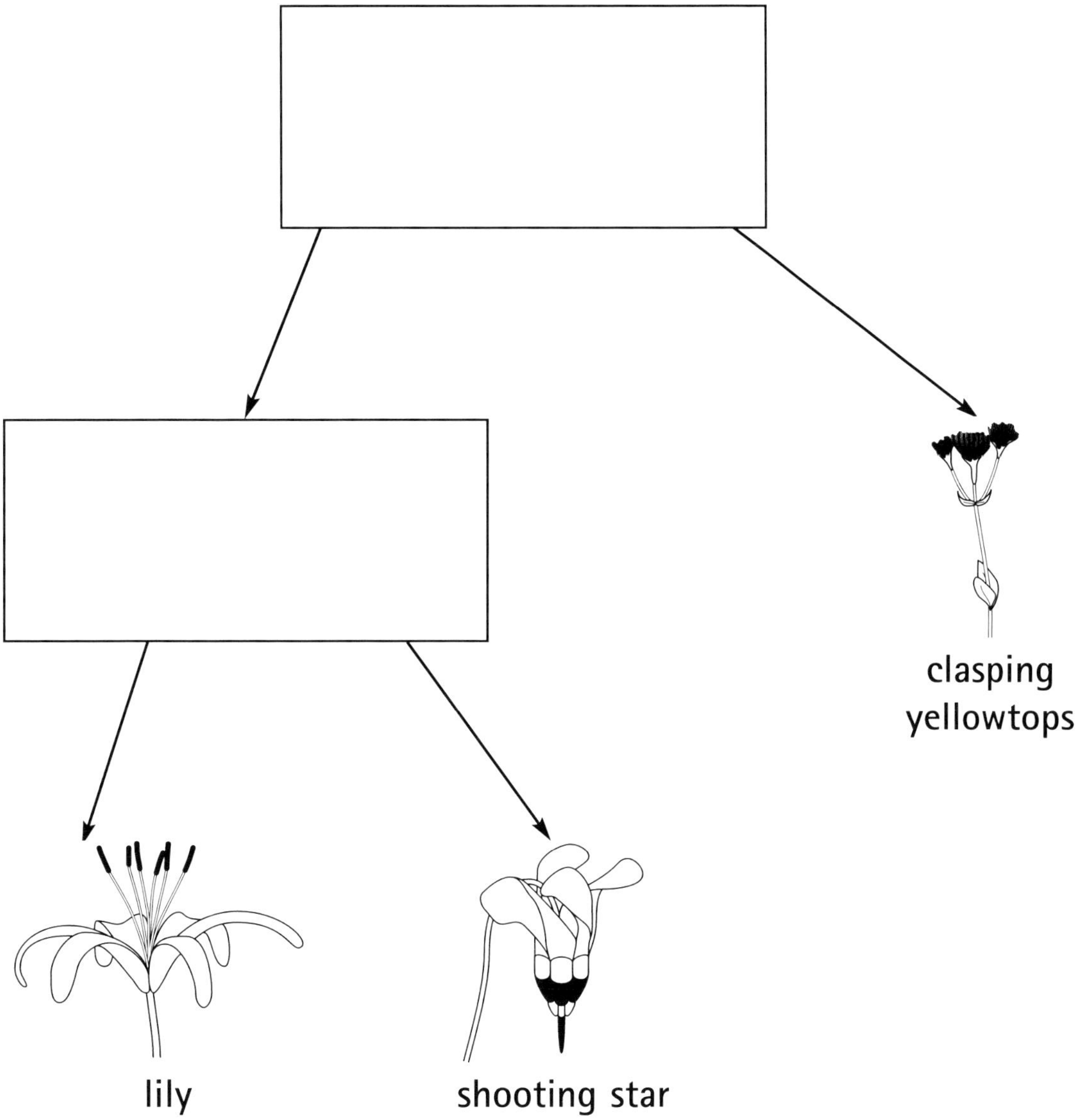

a) Use the following list to write two questions in the correct boxes in the key.

- Do the petals stand upright?
- Are the petals large and round?
- Are the flowers single?

b) Write 'YES' and 'NO' in the correct places in the key.

5a
2 marks

5b
1 mark

/10
Total for this test

UNIT 6A
Interdependence and adaptation 2

Name:	Class:	Date:

1 A plant needs light to grow well.

a) Explain what the plant uses the light for.

______________________________ 1a 1 mark

b) Give two other things a plant needs so that it can grow well.

______________ and ______________ 1b 2 marks

2 Explain two ways a polar bear is suited to the Arctic environment.

i) ______________________________ 2 2 marks

ii) ______________________________

3 Why do farmers add fertiliser to the soil?

______________________________ 3 1 mark

4 a) Draw the three arrows in this food chain. 4a 1 mark

b) Join each animal to the correct labels. (Some may need joining to more than one label.) 4b 2 marks

predator	prey

c) Why is a plant essential to a food chain? 4c 1 mark

____

/10 Total for this test

UNIT 6A

Interdependence and adaptation 3

Name: ______________________ Class: __________ Date: __________

Class 6 pupils want to investigate how adding fertiliser to soil affects plant growth.

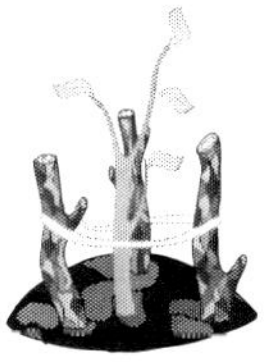

1. What question could they test?

   ____

   ____

   1 mark

2. What will they need to use?

   ____

   1 mark

3. What variable do they need to change in their test?

   ____

   1 mark

4. Name three things they need to keep the same to help make their test fair.

   i) ____________________ ii) ____________________

   iii) ____

   3 marks

5. What will they measure each day? ____________________

   1 mark

6. What equipment could they use to measure it? ____________________

   1 mark

7. Why would they use more than one plant in each condition?

   ____

   1 mark

8. How could they present their results? ____________________

   ____

   1 mark

/10 Total for this test

UNIT 6B

Micro-organisms 1

Name:	Class:	Date:

☺ 😐 ☹

1 a) What do germs cause? ____________________ 1a — 1 mark

b) How big are germs? Tick the correct box. 1b — 1 mark

- ☐ the size of a grain of sand
- ☐ the size of a small insect
- ☐ too small to see
- ☐ the size of a tadpole

2 How does cleaning your teeth regularly help prevent tooth decay? 2 — 2 marks

____

____

3 Give two good uses of micro-organisms. 3 — 2 marks

i) ____________________

ii) ____________________

4 Give two bad effects of micro-organisms. 4 — 2 marks

i) ____________________

ii) ____________________

5 Why should cooked and raw foods be kept apart? 5 — 2 marks

____

____

____

/10 Total for this test

UNIT 6B

Micro-organisms 2

Name:	Class:	Date:

1. All living creatures grow. Name two other things that all living creatures do. 1 — 2 marks

_______________ and _______________

2. a) Circle the things that decay. 2a — 2 marks

b) What causes things to decay? 2b — 1 mark

____

3. Name two foods that are produced using micro-organisms. 3 — 2 marks

_______________ and _______________

4. a) What three things do micro-organisms need to grow well on food? 4a — 1 mark

_______________ _______________ _______________

b) Describe two ways to stop food going mouldy. 4b — 2 marks

i) _______________

ii) _______________

/10 Total for this test

UNIT 6B
Micro-organisms 3

Name: Class: Date:

1 Connor has some yeast and wants to investigate the conditions that make it grow the most quickly. What question could he test?

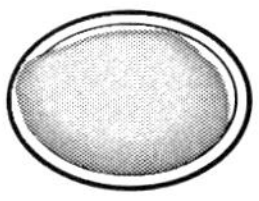
yeast

____

____

1 mark

2 What variable does he need to change in his test?

____

1 mark

3 Name three things Connor needs to keep the same to help make the test fair.

i) ______________________________

ii) ______________________________

iii) ______________________________

3 marks

4 What will he be measuring?

____

1 mark

5 What will he use to measure it? ______________________________

1 mark

6 How can he check the results of his test?

____

1 mark

7 Predict the conclusion of his test.

____

____

2 marks

/10 Total for this test

UNIT 6C

More about dissolving 1

Name: Class: Date:

☺ 😐 ☹

1 Ravinder mixes some powders with water. Circle the solutions.

(1) 2 marks

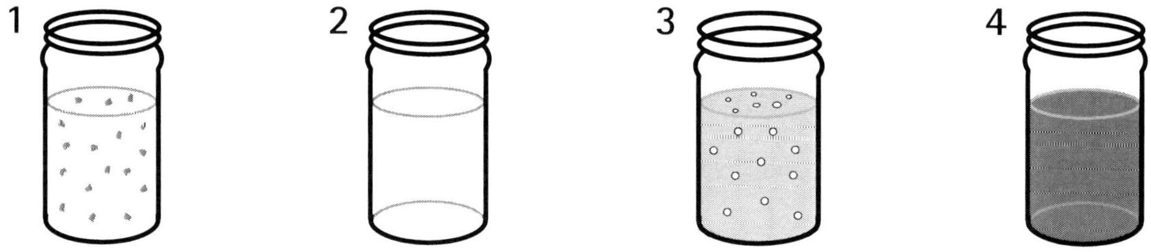

2 a) Name one solid that dissolves. ______________________

(2a) 1 mark

b) Solids that cannot dissolve are called ______________________.

(2b) 1 mark

3 A solid completely dissolves to form a solution.
Why can't you separate the solution using a filter?

(3) 1 mark

____

____

4 Peter mixes salt, sand and water.
How can he separate his mixture?

(4) 3 marks

____

____

____

5 The sea is salty.
Why is rainwater not salty?

(5) 2 marks

____

____

____

____

/10 Total for this test

UNIT 6C
More about dissolving 2

Name:	Class:	Date:

☺ 😐 ☹

(1) a) Circle the two solids that will dissolve in water. — 1a, 2 marks

salt   sand   sugar   flour

b) When a solid dissolves in a liquid, it makes a ________________. — 1b, 1 mark

c) Where does the dissolved solid go? — 1c, 1 mark

____

(2) Ali mixes a powder with water. It doesn't dissolve.

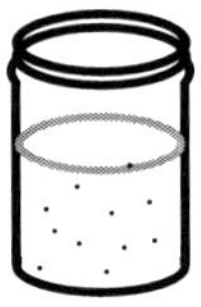

a) How can he separate this mixture? — 2a, 1 mark

____

b) How does that work? — 2b, 1 mark

____

____

(3) Describe how to separate a solid and liquid that form a solution. — 3, 2 marks

____

____

(4) Becky puts some fizzy orange and some ice cubes in a glass.
She notices drops of liquid appearing on the outside of the glass.

a) Name the process that causes liquid to appear on the outside of the glass. — 4a, 1 mark

____

b) What colour will this liquid be? — 4b, 1 mark

____

/10 Total for this test

UNIT 6C
More about dissolving 3

Name: Class: Date:

☺ 😐 ☹

1 Ella wants to investigate what affects the time it takes salt to dissolve in a beaker of water. What question could she test?

1 mark

2 What variable does she need to change in her test?

1 mark

3 Name two things she needs to keep the same to help make the test fair.

i)

ii)

2 marks

4 What will Ella be measuring?

1 mark

5 What will she use to measure it?

1 mark

6 How can she check the results of her test?

1 mark

7 How should Ella record her results?

1 mark

8 Predict the conclusion of her test.

2 marks

/10 Total for this test

UNIT 6D

Reversible and irreversible changes 1

Name: Class: Date:

1 Amy puts three different powders into three beakers of water.
Match the beaker or beakers to the sentences in the table.
(One of them has been done for you.)

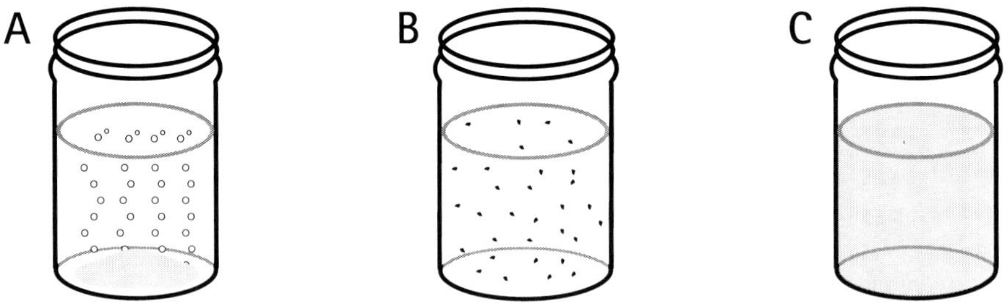

It has made a solution.	
It has bubbles in it.	A
It can be separated by filtering.	
It cannot be separated by filtering.	
It can only be separated by evaporation.	
It is making a gas.	
You can still see the powder.	
It is a chemical change.	

1 — 5 marks

2 a) Is burning a reversible change? YES NO

b) Give a reason for your answer.

____

____

2a — 1 mark

2b — 1 mark

3 Complete the following table.

	What happens when heated?
butter	
water	
egg	

3 — 3 marks

/10 Total for this test

UNIT 6D
Reversible and irreversible changes 2

Name: Class: Date:

1 Mrs Callow is conducting a test to see how different materials burn in a candle flame.

Give three ways in which she could make the test safe.

i) ______________________________

ii) ______________________________

iii) ______________________________

1 — 3 marks

2 Name two new materials that are made when paper burns.

______________ and ______________

2 — 2 marks

3 a) Circle those materials that will burn in a candle flame.

cotton wool

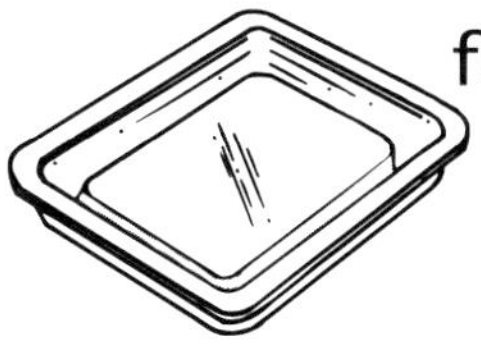

foil dish

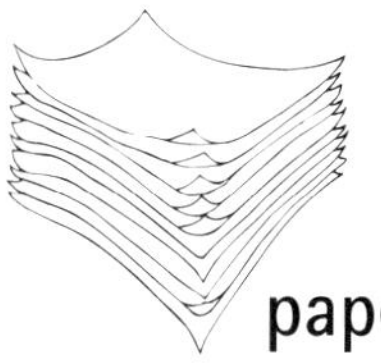

paper

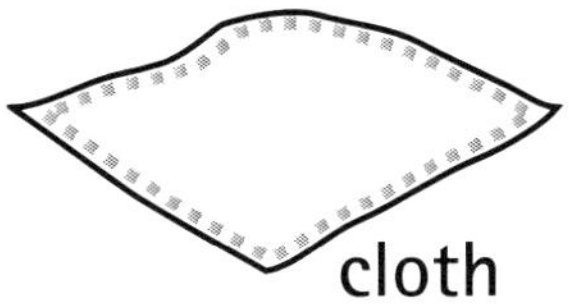

cloth

2p coin

3a — 2 marks

b) Name one other material that will burn in a candle flame.

____

3b — 1 mark

4 a) What is the process of changing from a solid to a liquid called?

____

4a — 1 mark

b) What is the process of changing from a liquid to a solid called?

____

4b — 1 mark

/10 Total for this test

UNIT 6D
Reversible and irreversible changes 3

Name: Class: Date:

☺ 😐 ☹

(1) Carys is investigating how the strength of plaster of Paris is affected by the amount of water that is mixed with the plaster powder.

1 [ ] 1 mark

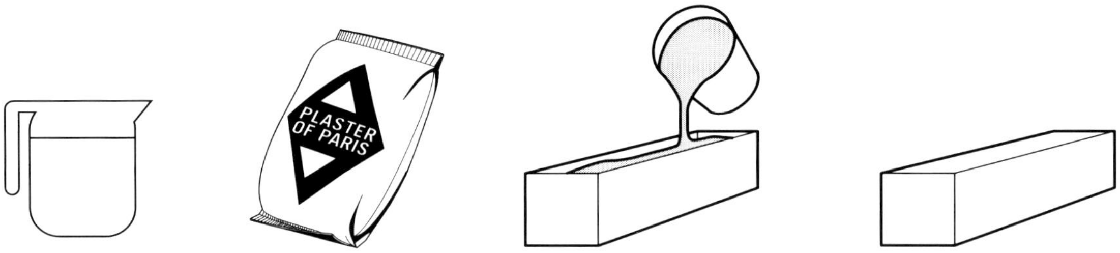

block of plaster of Paris

What variable does she need to change in her test?

____

(2) Name three things she needs to keep the same to help make the test fair.

2 [ ] 3 marks

i) ____

ii) ____

iii) ____

(3) What will Carys be measuring?

3 [ ] 1 mark

____

(4) Give one way that she could measure this.

4 [ ] 1 mark

____

[ ] Total for this page

Reversible and irreversible changes 3

(5) How can Carys check the results of her test?

____

____

1 mark 5

(6) She puts her results in a graph.

Morgan says, 'More water makes plaster stronger'.

Is he correct? YES NO

1 mark 6

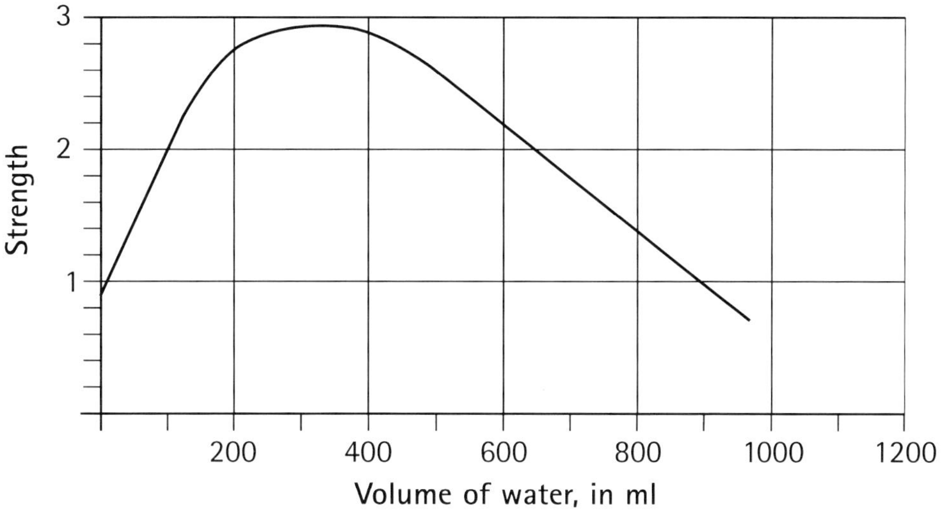

(7) How does the graph show this?

____

____

1 mark 7

(8) Mark on the graph where the plaster is strongest.

1 mark 8

/10 Total for this test

UNIT 6E

Forces in action 1

Name:	Class:	Date:

☺ 😐 ☹

1 Savas is measuring pulls. He uses the apparatus shown in the picture.

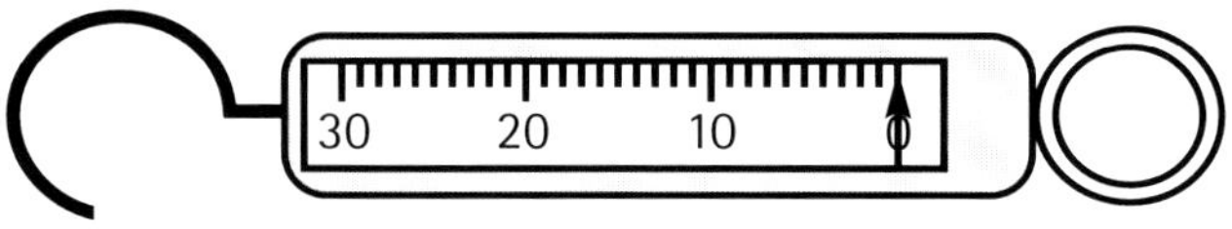

a) What is it called?

______________________ 1a 1 mark

b) What units do we use to measure force? ______________________ 1b 1 mark

2 Circle the forces. 2 1 mark

weight height gravity friction

3 a) Draw arrows to show the directions of two forces in this diagram. 3a 1 mark

b) Label each arrow. 3b 1 mark

4 a) Carys weighs some objects both in the air and then in water.

i) A stone weighs 9 N in air.
What will Carys observe when she weighs it in water?

______________________ 4ai 1 mark

ii) A metal hoop weighs 4 N in water.
What will Carys observe when she weighs it in air?

______________________ 4aii 1 mark

b) Give a reason for your answers.

______________________ 4b 1 mark

5 a) What does air resistance do to a plane?

______________________ 5a 1 mark

b) How is a plane designed to reduce the effects of air resistance?

______________________ 5b 1 mark

/10 Total for this test

UNIT 6E

Forces in action 2

Name:	Class:	Date:

1 Draw arrows from the people to show the direction in which gravity acts.

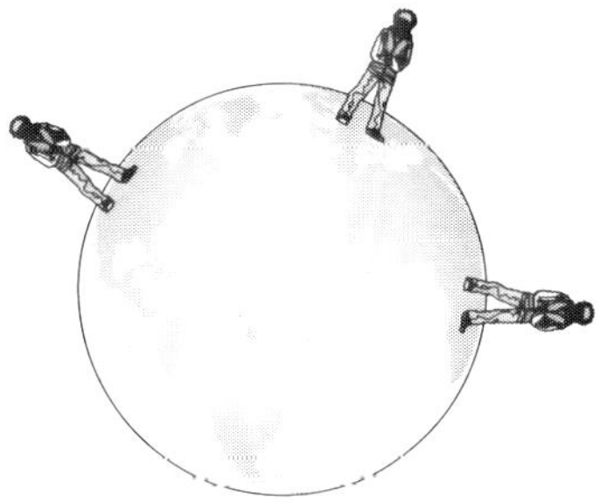

1 mark

2 A space team weighs a sack on Earth and on the Moon.

The weights are: **Earth 36 N** **Moon 6 N**

Explain why the weights are different.

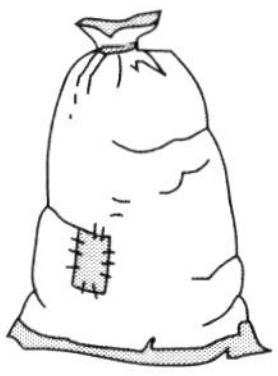

____

1 mark

3 Write down the reading on this forcemeter. (Include the units.)

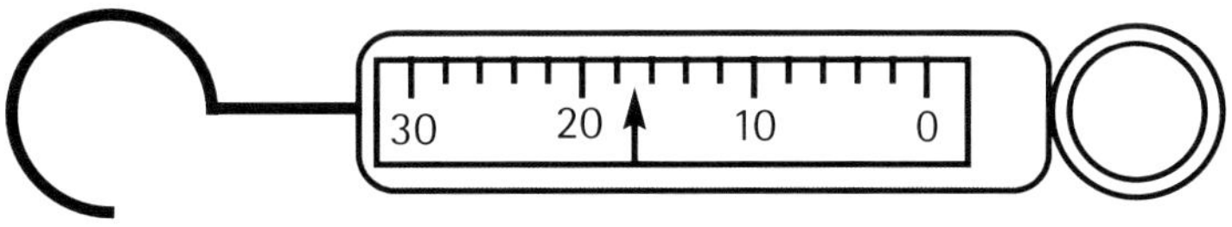

2 marks

4 Draw labelled arrows to show two forces on the diagram.

3 marks

5 A speed boat is travelling on the sea. Complete the table to describe the role of the forces.

Force	Role
Push from motor	Drives the boat forwards
Gravity	
Upthrust from water	
Water resistance	

3 marks

/10 Total for this test

UNIT 6E

Forces in action 3

Name: Class: Date:

☺ 😐 ☹

1 Class 6 pupils want to investigate the effect of weighing objects in water. What question could they test?

1 mark

2 Circle the pieces of equipment that they will need to use.

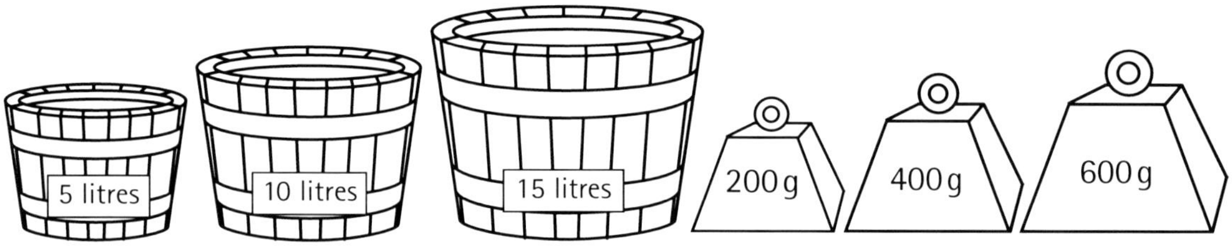

1 mark

3 What variable will they change in their test?

1 mark

4 Name two things they need to keep the same to help make the test fair.

i)

ii)

2 marks

5 What will they be measuring?

1 mark

6 What will they use to measure it?

1 mark

7 How can they check their results?

1 mark

8 Why do they need to check their results?

1 mark

9 How could they present their results?

1 mark

/10 Total for this test

UNIT 6F

How we see things 1

Name:	Class:	Date:

1 a) Draw the shadow from the sign.

b) Why is a shadow formed?

____

1a — 1 mark
1b — 1 mark

2 Circle the object or objects that make a dark shadow.

stone tracing paper glass

2 — 1 mark

3 a) Draw arrows to show how the light travels to and away from the mirror.

torch

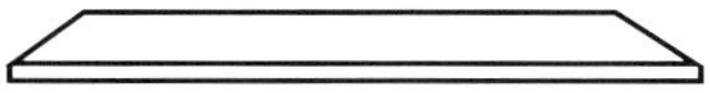

mirror

3a — 2 marks

b) Min shines a torch on a pot. Describe one way she can change the size of the shadow.

____

____

3b — 1 mark

c) Light from the Sun lets the man see the car. Draw arrows to show how the man sees the car.

3c — 2 marks

4 How is a shadow different from a reflection?

____

____

____

4 — 2 marks

/10 Total for this test

UNIT 6F

How we see things 2

Name: Class: Date:

1 Complete the following sentences.

a) We see an object because ______________ from the object ______________________________ .

b) You get a shadow when ______________________________ .

2 a) Tick the drawing with the correct shadow.

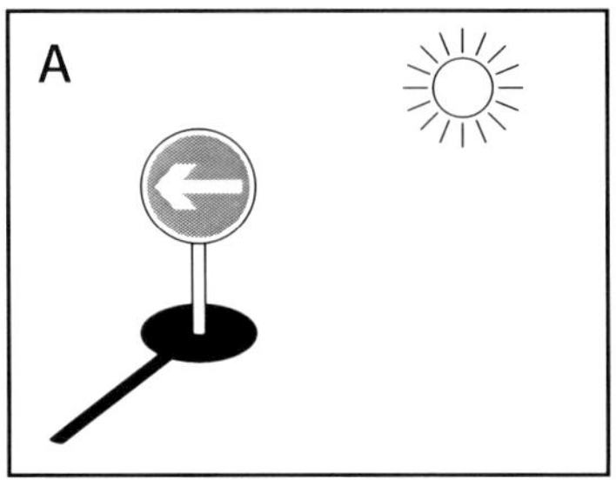

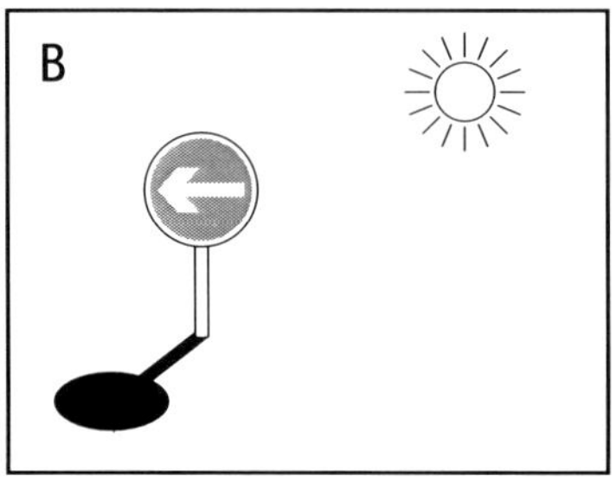

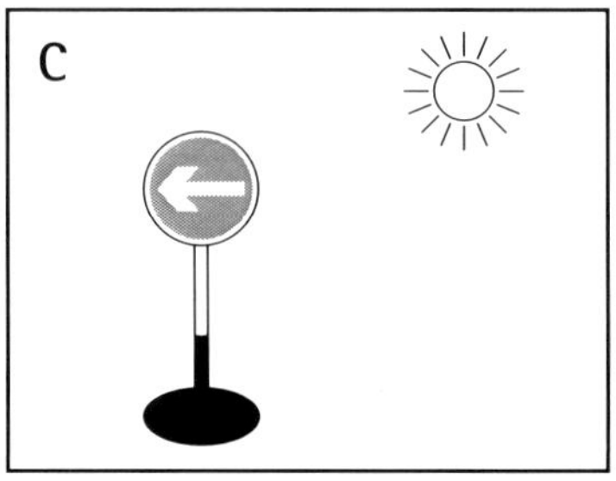

b) Circle the word that completes the following sentence correctly.

The signpost is **opaque** **transparent** **translucent**

3 The light lets the boy see the door in the mirror. Draw three arrows to show how the boy sees the door.

4 Why does a silver necklace look shiny?

____

5 a) Draw arrows to show how light travels between the torch and the mirror and how the light reflects.

b) A reflection is when light ______________ a shiny surface, but a shadow is made when an opaque object ______________ light.

1a 1 mark

1b 1 mark

2a 1 mark

2b 1 mark

3 2 marks

4 1 mark

5a 2 marks

5b 1 mark

/10 Total for this test

UNIT 6F

How we see things 3

Name: Class: Date:

☺ 😐 ☹

1 Tom wants to investigate ways in which shadow size changes. What question could he test?

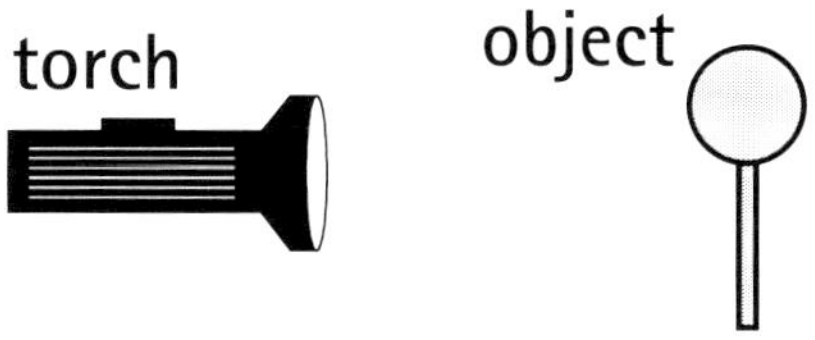

____

____

1 mark

2 What variable does he need to change in his test?

____

1 mark

3 Name two variables he needs to keep the same to help make the test fair.

____________________ and ____________________

1 mark

4 Which two variables will he measure?

____________________ and ____________________

2 marks

5 What equipment could he use to measure these? ____________________

1 mark

6 How can he check the results of his test?

____

1 mark

7 Tom decides to use a line graph to record his results. Explain why this is a good choice.

____

____

1 mark

8 Predict the conclusion of his test.

____

____

2 marks

/10 Total for this test

UNIT 6G

Changing circuits 1

Name: Class: Date:

① Tick the circuit that will light a bulb.

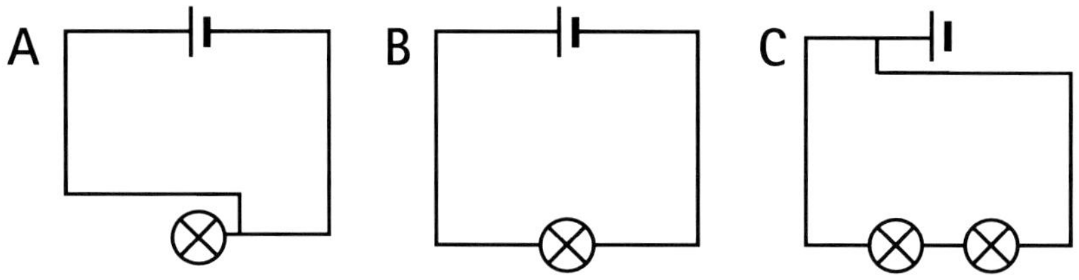

1 mark (1)

② a) Draw the symbol for a bulb.

1 mark (2a)

b) Draw the symbol for a wire.

1 mark (2b)

c) What is the function of a switch?

___

1 mark (2c)

③ Min constructs a circuit to make her toy roundabout spin.

a) Use the correct symbols to draw the circuit she used.

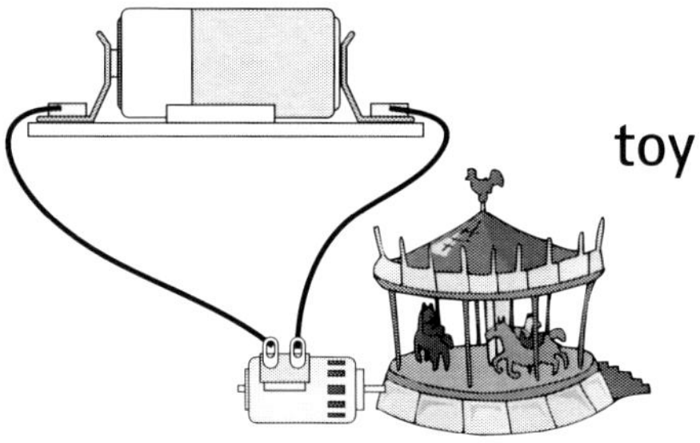

1 mark (3a)

b) How could she make the roundabout go faster?

___

1 mark (3b)

④ Circle the items that are conductors of electricity.

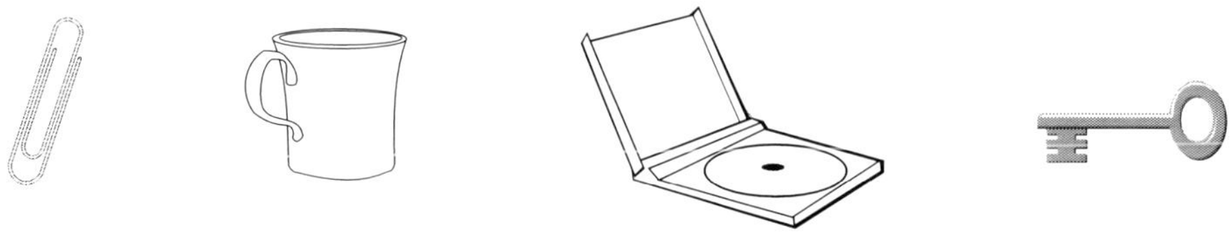

2 marks (4)

⑤ Explain why electrical wires have plastic covers.

___

___

2 marks (5)

/10 Total for this test

UNIT 6G
Changing circuits 2

Name: Class: Date:

1 Tick the circuits that will work. *(1 mark)*

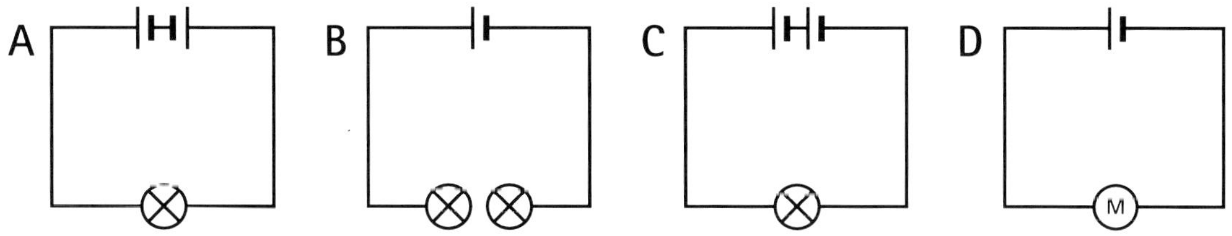

2 Explain the meaning of the following symbols: *(2 marks)*

means ______________________________

means ______________________________

means ______________________________

3 Draw a circuit with two cells, a motor, a bulb and a switch. *(2 marks)*

4 What is the job of a cell? ______________________________ *(1 mark)*

5 Which group of materials are good electrical conductors? *(1 mark)*

____

6 Why is it safe to conduct experiments with batteries but not with mains electricity? *(1 mark)*

____

7 Describe how a switch works. *(2 marks)*

____

____

/10 Total for this test

UNIT 6G
Changing circuits 3

Name:	Class:	Date:

1 Ravinder wants to investigate how different sizes of wire can affect the brightness of a bulb. What question could she test?

____

____

1 mark

2 Ravinder has a bulb and a battery. Circle the wires she needs.

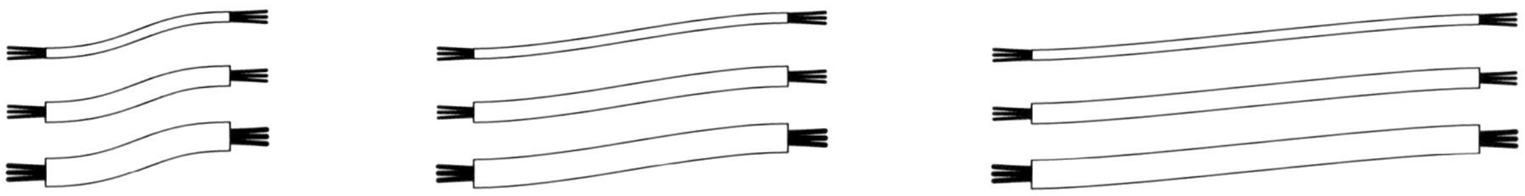

1 mark

3 What variable does she need to change in her test?

____

1 mark

4 Name two things she needs to keep the same to help make the test fair.

i) ____

ii) ____

2 marks

5 What will she be measuring? ______________________________

1 mark

6 What could she use to measure it? ______________________________

1 mark

7 How can she check the results of her test?

____

1 mark

8 Predict the conclusion of her test.

____

____

2 marks

/10 Total for this test

UNIT 6A
Interdependence and adaptation 4

Name: Class: Date:

1 a) Sam is investigating leaves.
How do leaves help a green plant to grow?

1a — 1 mark

b) Sam is using plants in a test. She chooses three plants that are the same type and size. Explain why.

1b — 1 mark

She strips some leaves from some of the plants. She then measures the height of the plants each week for three weeks.
She records her results.

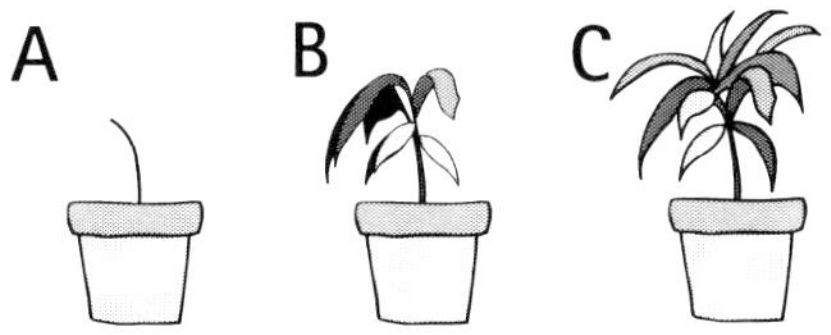

	Height, in cm		
	Week 1	Week 2	Week 3
Plant A	8	8	8
Plant B	8	11	10
Plant C	8	9	11.5

c) Circle the measurement that seems wrong.

1c — 1 mark

d) Explain why this result seems to be wrong.

1d — 2 marks

Sam keeps all the plants in the same place and gives them the same amount of water. After four weeks she draws her plants.

e) How has plant A changed?

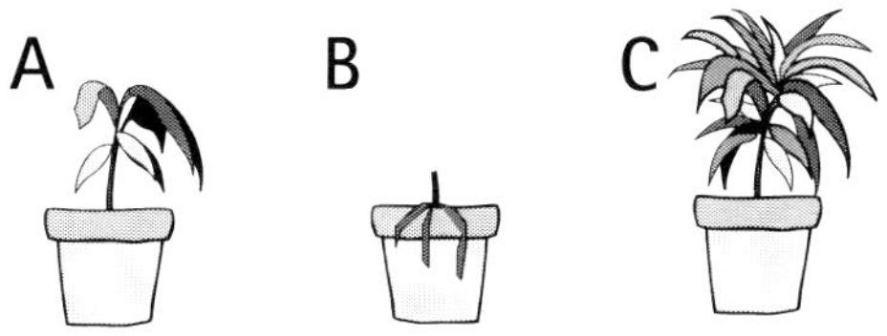

1e — 1 mark

f) Sam's teacher says she should have used more than one plant in each group. Explain why.

1f — 1 mark

Total for this page

UNIT 6A

Interdependence and adaptation 4

☺ 😐 ☹

2 Clay soils are heavy, sticky and drain slowly.
Sandy soils are light and drain quickly.

a) Give two reasons why this plant is suited to clay soil.

i) ______________________________

ii) ______________________________

2a
2 marks

b) Draw in roots that are suited to sandy soil.

2b
1 mark

/10
Total for this test

UNIT 6B
Micro-organisms 4

Name: Class: Date:

☺ 😐 ☹

(1) Becky is testing how much mould grows on strawberries at different temperatures.

a) Give two things Becky needs to keep the same to help make her test fair.

i) ______________________________

ii) ______________________________

1a
2 marks

b) Draw arrows to match each of these strawberries with the temperature at which it was stored for one week.

1b
1 mark

8°C	2°C	15°C

c) What conclusion can you draw from this investigation of temperature and growth of mould on strawberries?

____

____

1c
2 marks

d) Give one piece of evidence that the mould is living.

____

____

1d
1 mark

Total for this page

UNIT 6B
Micro-organisms 4

2) Complete the sentence.

To grow well, microbes need warmth, ______________________________

and ______________________________ .

2 — 1 mark

3) Look at the chart.

	Yeast	Yeast and sugar
Start	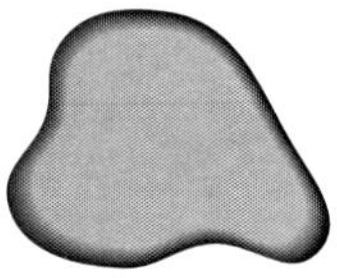	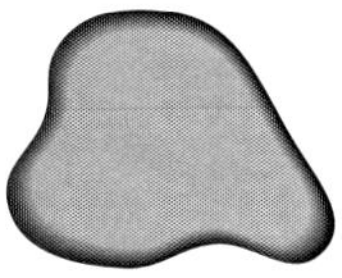
After two hours	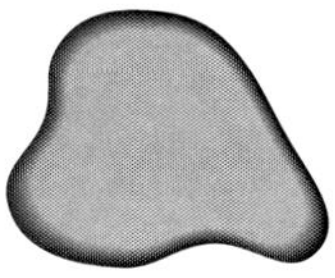	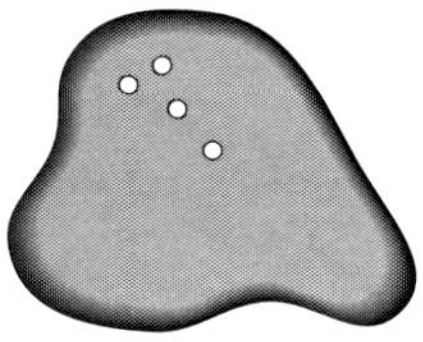

a) The bubbles on the larger piece of yeast show that it is making

______________________________ .

3a — 1 mark

b) Give two pieces of evidence that yeast is living.

i) ______________________________

ii) ______________________________

3b — 2 marks

/10 Total for this test

UNIT 6C

More about dissolving 4

Name: Class: Date:

1 Daniel is testing how the temperature of water affects the time it takes to dissolve salt.

a) Give two things he needs to keep the same to help make his test fair.

i) ______________________

ii) ______________________

1a 2 marks

He puts his results in a table.

Temperature of water	Time taken to dissolve, in seconds		
	1st try	2nd try	3rd try
20°C	360	348	356
30°C	121	130	180
40°C	19	21	21

b) Circle the reading that seems to be wrong.

1b 1 mark

c) Daniel has two or more accurate results for each temperature. How does he work out the measurements to plot on his graph?

____

____

1c 1 mark

d) Continue the line on Daniel's graph to show what happens at higher temperatures.

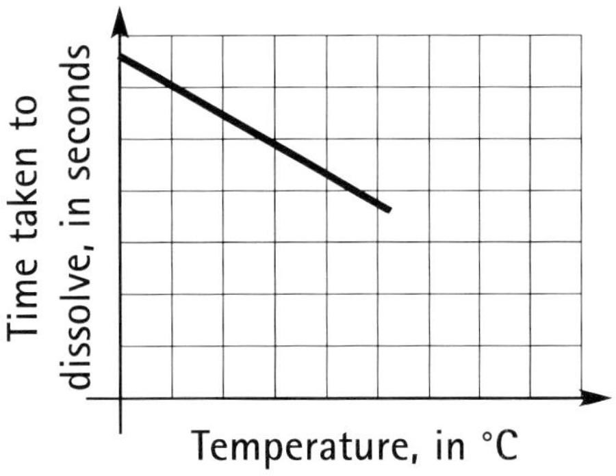

1d 1 mark

e) What conclusion can Daniel draw?

____

____

1e 2 marks

f) How can Daniel get the dissolved salt back again?

____

____

1f 1 mark

Total for this page

UNIT 6C
More about dissolving 4

☺ 😐 ☹

(2) Min puts some powder into a beaker of acid.
The mixture starts to bubble.

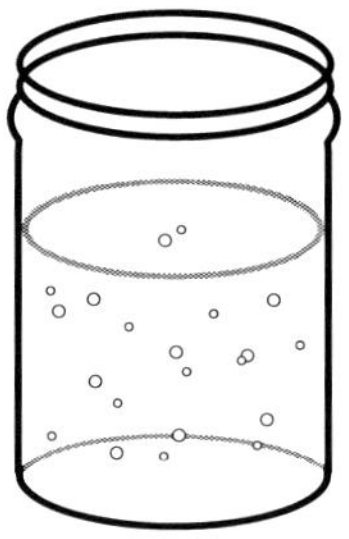

a) What could cause the bubbles to appear?

____

____

2a
1 mark

b) What might be in the bubbles?

____

2b
1 mark

/10
Total for this test

Reversible and irreversible changes 4

Name: Class: Date:

1) Savas is testing the effect of adding different amounts of bicarbonate of soda to vinegar. He puts the bicarbonate of soda in a balloon and fixes the balloon to the bottle of vinegar. He tips the bicarbonate of soda into the vinegar.

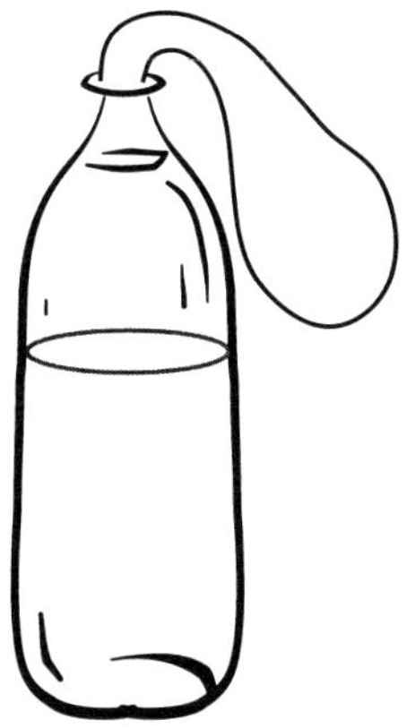

a) What does he change in his test?

______________________________ 1a 1 mark

b) Give two things he might keep the same to help make his test fair.

i) ______________________________

ii) ______________________________ 1b 2 marks

c) How will he be able to tell which amount has made the most gas?

____

______________________________ 1c 1 mark

d) Is the change reversible? YES NO 1d 1 mark

e) What is the evidence for this?

____

______________________________ 1e 1 mark

Total for this page

UNIT 6D

Reversible and irreversible changes 4

(2) Carys is testing the temperature at which different solids turn to liquids.

a) What is the process of changing from a solid to a liquid called?

____

2a
1 mark

b) What is the reverse process called?

____

2b
1 mark

She puts her results into a table.

Type of solid	Temperature at which the solid turns to liquid, in °C
ice	1
butter	29
chocolate	37

c) Ella says, 'You have to heat things above room temperature to change them to liquids'. Which solid in the table does not fit Ella's rule?

____

2c
1 mark

d) If you heat ice, it changes to a liquid. What then happens if you keep heating the liquid?

____

2d
1 mark

/10
Total for this test

Forces in action 4

Name: Class: Date:

☺ 😐 ☹

1 a) Amy and Bart are testing the falling times of different diameter parachutes. Give one way they can make their test fair.

1a
1 mark

b) They put their results in a table.

Circle the reading that seems odd.

	Falling time, in seconds		
Diameter of parachute	1st try	2nd try	3rd try
15 cm parachute	9	11	10
20 cm parachute	12	13	8
25 cm parachute	16	17	16

1b
1 mark

c) Why do they do each test three times?

1c
1 mark

d) They have more than one result for each parachute. How do they work out what to plot on their graph?

1d
1 mark

They make a graph of their correct results.

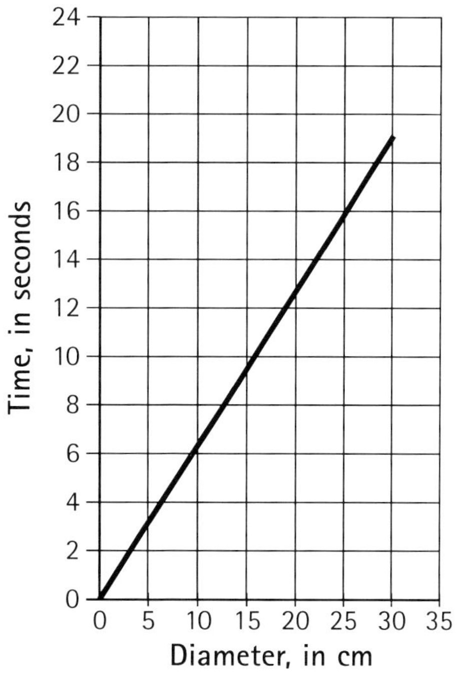

e) How many seconds will it take a 35 cm parachute to fall?

1e
1 mark

Total for this page

UNIT 6E
Forces in action 4

f) What conclusion can you draw from their graph?

____

____

____

1f
2 marks

g) How does the graph show this?

____

____

____

1g
1 mark

h) Add two arrows to the drawing to show two forces on the parachute as it falls.

Name each force.

1h
2 marks

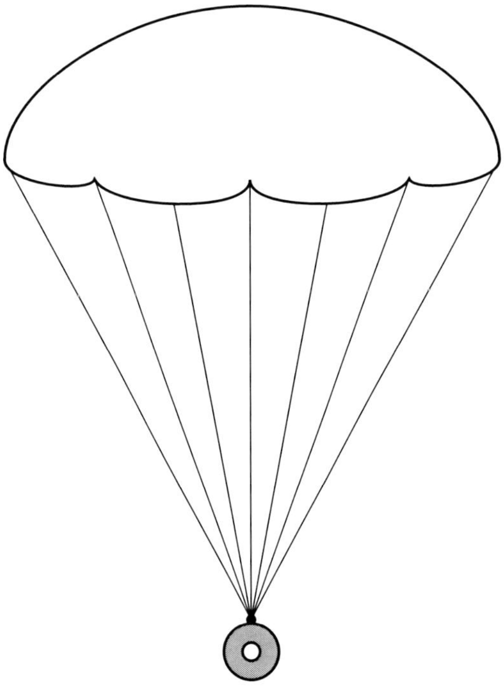

/10
Total for this test

UNIT 6F

How we see things 4

Name: Class: Date:

☺ 😐 ☹

1. Sam and Morgan are measuring the angle light hits a mirror and is reflected from the mirror.

a) What should they use to measure the angle?

____

1a
1 mark

b) Why does a mirror reflect light?

____

1b
1 mark

They put their results in a table.

Angle light hits mirror	21°	29°	40°	50°
Angle light reflected from mirror	20°	30°	24°	50°

c) Circle the reading that is incorrect.

1c
1 mark

d) What do you think the reading should be? ______________

1d
1 mark

e) How can they check their results?

____

____

1e
1 mark

f) What do the results show?

____

____

1f
1 mark

g) Add an arrow to this drawing Sam made to show how the light is reflected.

1g
1 mark

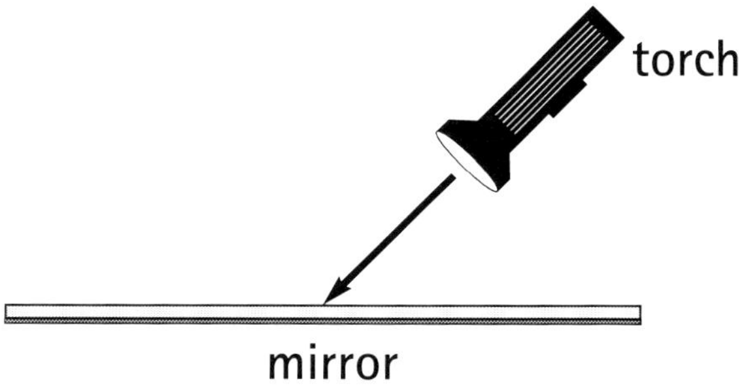

Total for this page

UNIT 6F
How we see things 4

(2) The pupils investigate the size of shadows.

2
1 mark

Who makes the tallest shadow on the wall? ______________________

(3) Add two arrows to this drawing to show how light lets Min see the glass containing a drink.

3
2 marks

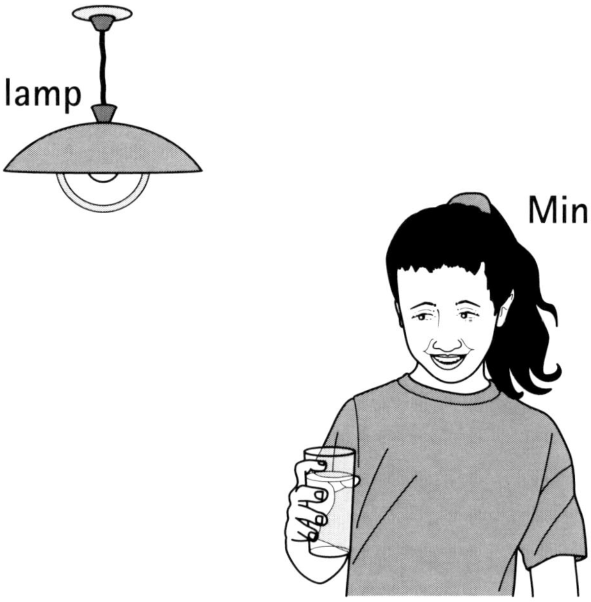

/10
Total for this test

UNIT 6G
Changing circuits 4

Name: Class: Date:

☺ 😐 ☹

1 Class 6 pupils are testing how the number of 1.5 V cells affects the brightness of a bulb. They use a circuit with one bulb.

a) Give two things they can do to help make their test fair.

i) ____________________

ii) ____________________

1a — 2 marks

b) What could they use to measure the brightness of the bulb?

____

1b — 1 mark

They plot their results.

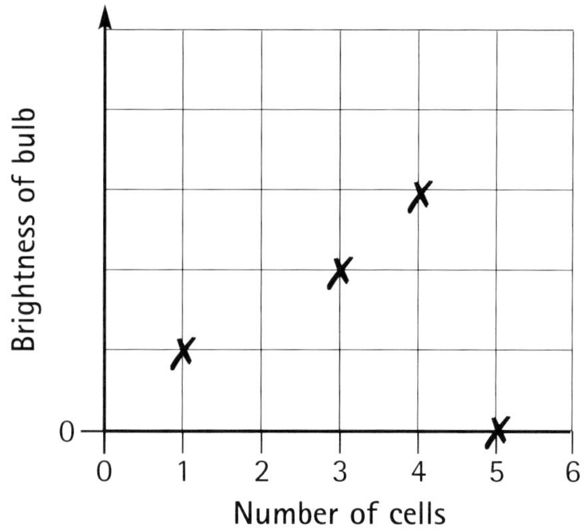

c) Plot the points for two cells and for six cells on the graph.

1c — 2 marks

d) Explain why the reading is zero for five cells.

____

1d — 1 mark

e) What is the maximum voltage of the bulb that they used?

1e — 1 mark

f) What do their results show?

____

____

1f — 2 marks

Total for this page

C.ıanging circuits 4

☺ 😐 ☹

(2) The switch can be closed in two ways. Circle the bulb that will be on when the motor is running.

2

1 mark

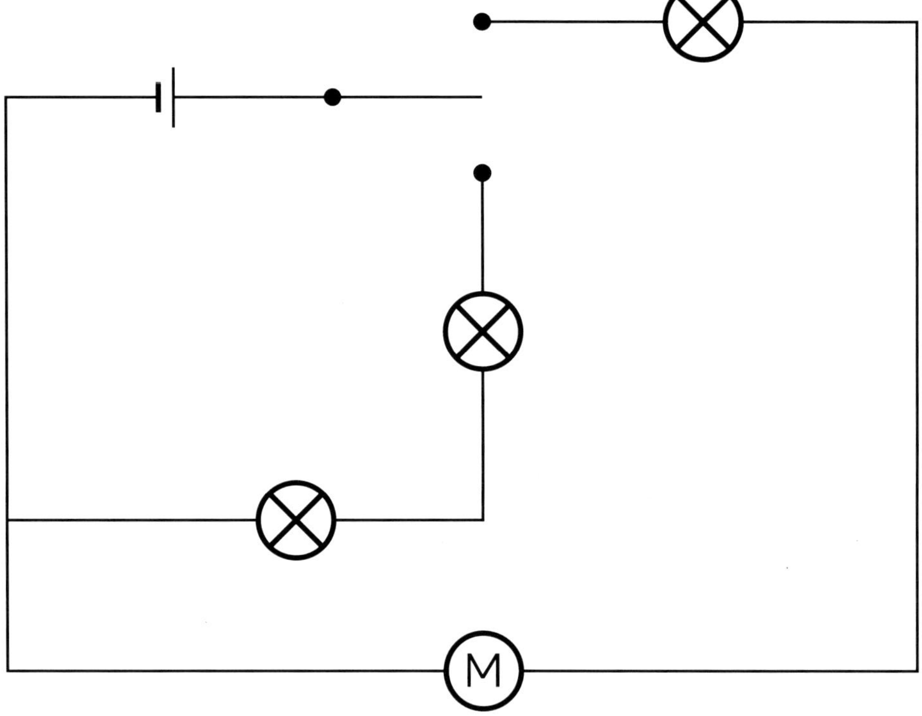

/10

Total for this test

Answers and mark schemes for Tests 1–3

6A 1	Interdependence and adaptation	Mark	Extra information
1	leaves will turn yellow	1	accept plant gets very tall do not accept plant dies
2	anchors or holds the plant in the ground absorbs or soaks up water	1 1	 accept absorbs minerals or nutrients
3 a b	leaves water/minerals/light/carbon dioxide	1 1	green parts two correct answers for 1 mark
4 a b	shelter or protection fertilising the soil or pollinating the plant or dispersing seeds	1 1	accept to hide in or make nests
5 a b	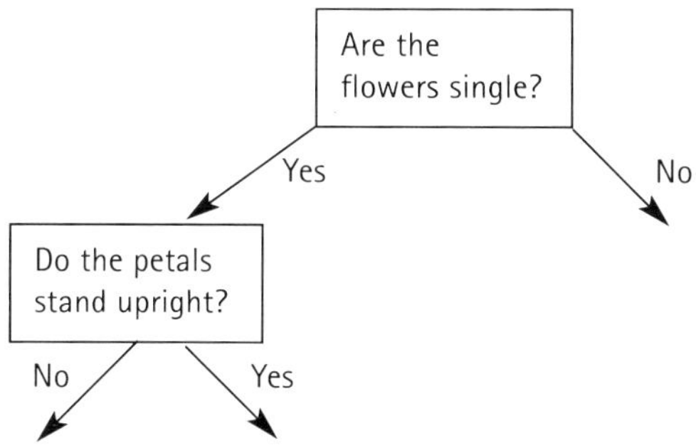 correct questions entered YES/NO all correct on the key	 2 1	

6A 2	Interdependence and adaptation	Mark	Extra information
1 a b	to make food **any two from:** water; air; nutrients	1 2	 allow soil
2	**any two from:** white fur for camouflage; large paws to stop sinking in the snow; layer of fat or thick fur to keep warm	2	attribute and use must both be given for each mark
3	to make crops or plants grow better/faster/stronger; or to add nutrients to the soil	1	
4 a b c	arrows facing right to left 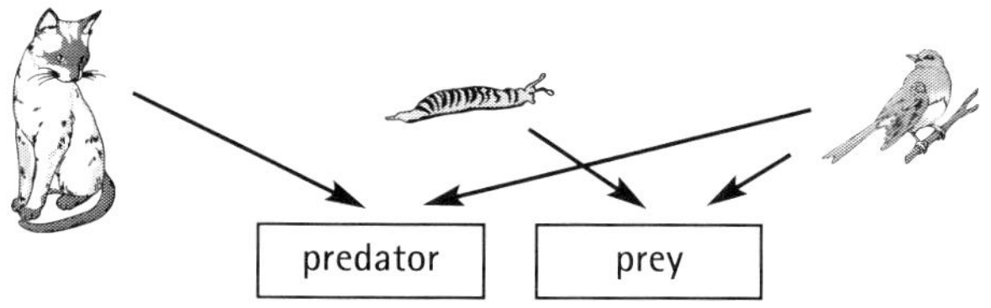 it is eaten by animals or it makes food from air and water and light	1 2 1	i.e. from lettuce through to cat all correct 2 marks two arrows correct 1 mark accept from light

6A 3	Interdependence and adaptation			Mark
1	how does the use of one fertiliser affect different plants?	how does the use of different fertilisers affect the growth of one type of plant?	how does the amount of fertiliser affect the growth of the plant?	1
2	one fertiliser and two/three plant types	one type of plant and two/three fertiliser types	one fertiliser and one type of plant	1
3	plant type	fertiliser type	amount of fertiliser	1
4	**any three from:** same place; same temperature; plant at the same time; same sized pots; same amount of water; same amount of fertiliser	**any three from:** same place; same temperature; plant at the same time; same sized pots; same amount of water; same amount of fertiliser	**any three from:** same place; same temperature; plant at the same time; same sized pots; same type of fertiliser; same type of plant; same amount of water	3
5	height/size of plant/amount of growth/weight			1
6	ruler, stick or weighing scales			1
7	in case some of the plants are diseased/unhealthy/die/do not grow properly; to check the test			1
8	graph/table/chart			1

6B 1	Micro-organisms	Mark	Extra information
1 a b	illness or disease too small to see	1 1	accept specific diseases tiny or minute
2	removes food/plaque on which harmful micro-organisms grow	2	removes micro-organisms/bacteria 1 mark
3	**any two from:** makes yoghurt/bread/cheese/alcohol/ginger beer/medicines; in compost; is yeast	2	
4	illness/disease rots food or decay	1 1	accept reference to misuse of alcohol
5	the micro-organisms that would be killed when the raw food is cooked could spread to cooked food and make it unsafe	2	raw foods have micro-organisms in them that spread to the cooked foods for 1 mark

6B 2	Micro-organisms	Mark	Extra information
1	**any two from:** reproduce; move; sense or feel; feed or make food; excrete; respire	2	accept take in air, but not breathe
2 a	paper, leaves and vegetables circled	2	all correct 2 marks two correct 1 mark deduct 1 mark for each item circled incorrectly
b	micro-organisms/microbes	1	
3	**any two from:** cheese; bread; yoghurt; beer or wine	2	accept ginger beer
4 a	water, warmth and air	1	all required for 1 mark
b	**any two from:** take the water away; take the air away; take the warmth away/freeze it	2	i.e. dried foods; tinned foods; frozen foods

6B 3	Micro-organisms			Mark
1	does the amount of sugar (or water) affect how much the yeast grows?	does the type of sugar affect how much the yeast grows?	does temperature affect how much the yeast grows?	1
2	the amount of sugar (or water)	the type of sugar	the temperature	1
3	**any three from:** same amount of yeast; same temperature; same time left; same place used; same type of sugar; same amount of sugar/water	**any three from:** same amount of yeast; same temperature; same time left; same place used; same amount of sugar; same amount of water	**any three from:** same amount of yeast; same time left; same place used; same amount or type of sugar; same amount of water	3
4	how much the yeast grows			1
5	scales/g/kg or ruler/height/cm or squared grid			1
6	do the test again or more than once or check with another group			1
7	2 marks for a double comparative relating to the question even if the prediction is incorrect, e.g. the more sugar there was, the more it grew 1 mark only for a single comparative, e.g. when there is a lot of sugar, it will grow bigger			2

6C 1	More about dissolving	Mark	Extra information
1	2 and 4 circled	2	
2 a b	sugar or salt, etc insoluble	1 1	any soluble solid
3	because it passes through the filter or the filter cannot hold the solid	1	
4	filter to remove the sand evaporate or boil off the water the salt is left in the dish	1 1 1	
5	because the salt does not evaporate there is only (pure) water in the clouds	1 1	 rain is condensed water that has evaporated

6C 2	More about dissolving	Mark	Extra information
1 a b c	salt and sugar circled solution goes into gaps in the liquid	2 1 1	 accept completely mixes with the liquid
2 a b	with a filter the filter has tiny holes that let the water through but won't let little pieces or solid through	1 1	
3	evaporate the liquid the solid is left in the dish	1 1	
4 a b	condensation colourless	1 1	 accept clear

6C 3	More about dissolving			Mark
1	does the temperature of the water affect how long it takes salt to dissolve?	does the amount of salt affect how long it takes salt to dissolve?	does the speed or amount of stirring affect how long it takes salt to dissolve?	1
2	the temperature of the water	the amount of salt	the speed or amount of stirring	1
3	any two from: same amount of water; same amount of salt; same amount and time of stirring; same type of salt	any two from: same amount of water; same temperature of water; same amount and time of stirring; same type of salt	any two from: same amount of water; same amount of salt; same temperature of water; same type of salt	2
4	time for all the salt to dissolve			1
5	stopwatch or clock			1
6	do the test again or more than once or check with another group			1
7	in a table or graph			1
8	2 marks for a double comparative relating to the question even if the prediction is incorrect, e.g. the more salt there was, the longer it took to dissolve 1 mark only for a single comparative, e.g. when there is more salt, it will dissolve slowly			2

6D 1	Reversible and irreversible changes		Mark	Extra information
1	It has made a solution.	C	5	all seven correct 5 marks
	It has bubbles in it.	[A]		deduct 1 mark for each error
	It can be separated by filtering.	A and B		both required
	It cannot be separated by filtering.	C		
	It can only be separated by evaporation.	C		
	It is making a gas.	A		
	You can still see the powder.	A and B		both required
	It is a chemical change.	A		
2 a	NO		1	accept 'YES' if photosynthesis is given as the opposite
b	new materials are made or it is a chemical change		1	
3	butter melts		1	
	water evaporates or boils		1	
	egg cooks or is chemical change		1	accept goes solid or hard

6D 2	Reversible and irreversible changes	Mark	Extra information
1	**any three from:** use tea light/low candle; use tongs to hold the material; put sand round the candle; put the candle in a dish; use special gloves	3	
2	ash or smoke carbon dioxide or gas	1 1	accept water
3 a b	cotton wool, cloth, paper anything else that will burn in a candle flame	2 1	all three correct 2 marks any two correct 1 mark
4 a b	melting freezing	1 1	 accept crystallising

6D 3	Reversible and irreversible changes	Mark	Extra information
1	the amount of water	1	
2	**any three from:** same amount of plaster; same temperature; same method of mixing; left for the same time to set; same mould	3	accept any three reasonable answers
3	the strength of the plaster or block	1	
4	weights or force to break it	1	
5	do the test again or compare the results with another group	1	
6	NO	1	
7	the strength increases as the water increases at first but then it gets less	1	an indication of a peaking required
8	highest point on the graph marked	1	

6E 1	Forces in action	Mark	Extra information
1 a b	forcemeter or newton meter newtons or N	1 1	
2	weight, gravity and friction all circled	1	all three correct for 1 mark
3 a b	arrows pointing in correct directions both arrows labelled correctly (gravity vertical, friction parallel with slide) 	1 1	arrows correct but no labels for 1 mark one arrow drawn and labelled for 1 mark
4 ai ii b	it will weigh less it will weigh more water upthrust supports the objects in water	1 1 1	 accept water partly supports the object
5 a b	slows it down or makes it harder to move/fly streamlined shape	1 1	

6E 2	Forces in action	Mark	Extra information
1	three arrows pointing towards the centre of the Earth	1	all three arrows required
2	the pull of gravity is less on the Moon	1	accept the converse
3	17 N or newtons	2	17 without unit 1 mark
4	arrow pointing vertically upwards, labelled air resistance; arrow pointing vertically downwards, labelled gravity or weight	3	all four correct 3 marks deduct 1 mark for each error
5	gravity: pulls the boat down/to the centre of the Earth/on the water water upthrust: holds the boat up on the water/stops it sinking or pushes up on boat water resistance: slows the boat down/works against the movement	1 1 1	 water resistance provides friction

6E 3	Forces in action			Mark
1	does the amount of water affect the weight?	do objects weigh the same in air and water?	is the link (ratio) between air and water readings related to the weight?	1
2	two or three different tubs of water and one weight	two or three different weights and one tub of water	two or three different weights and one tub of water	1
3	amount of water	weight used	weight used	1
4	**any two from:** same temperature of water; same weight; same shaped tubs	**any two from:** same temperature of water; weights made of same material; same amount of water	**any two from:** same temperature of water; weights made of same material; same amount of water, same shaped tubs	2
5	weight of object in and out of water; both required			1
6	forcemeter or N or newton meter			1
7	do the test again or more than once or check with another group			1
8	to get more reliable/average results or forcemeters difficult to read or reduce errors			1
9	graph or table or chart			1

6F 1	How we see things	Mark	Extra information
1 a	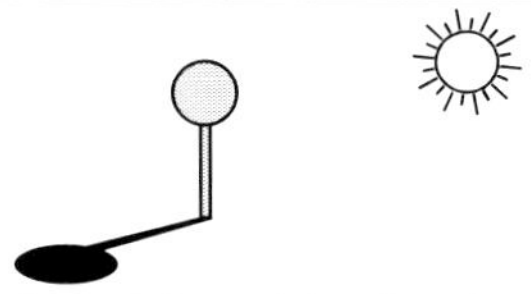	1	the direction is important, not the shape and should be between 'half past' and 'quarter to'
b	the object blocks the light from the Sun	1	blocks or stops must be in the answer
2	stone	1	
3 a	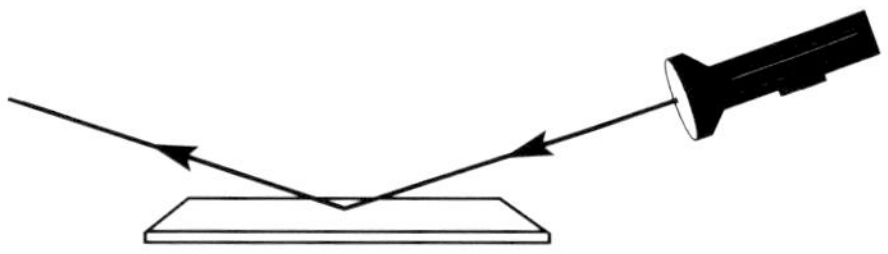 two lines drawn at approximately correct angles two arrows pointing from right to left	1 1	one arrow completely correct for 1 mark
b	move the pot closer or further away or raise or lower the torch	1	move the torch closer or further away
c	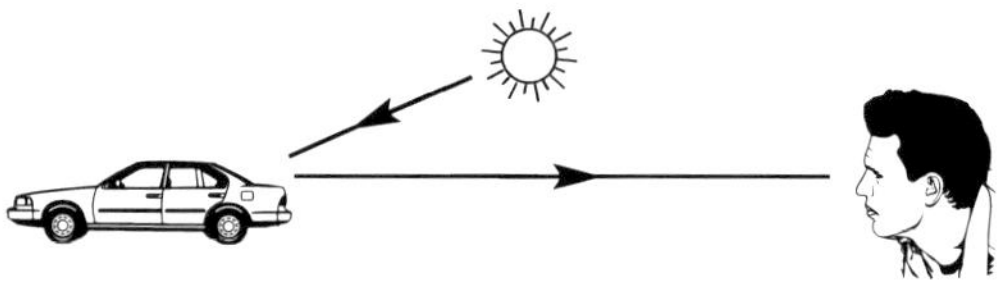 two lines drawn at correct angles two arrows pointing correctly	1 1	one arrow completely correct for 1 mark
4	a shadow is formed where material blocks out the light or is an absence of light a reflection is formed by light bouncing off or shining off a surface/mirror	1 1	

6F 2	How we see things	Mark	Extra information
1 a	light [from the object] enters our eyes or reaches our eyes	1	
b	the light is blocked	1	
2 a	shadow B	1	
b	opaque	1	
3	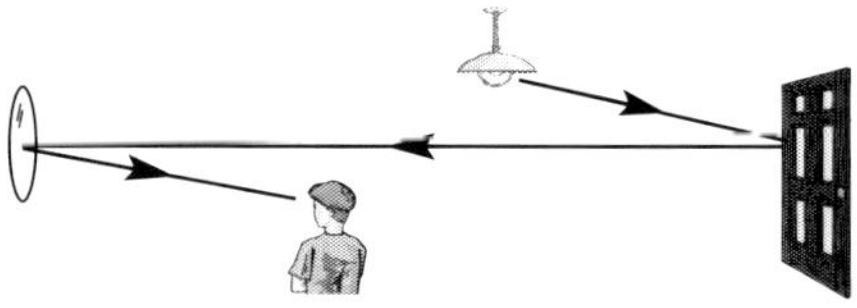 two lines drawn in correctly three arrows pointing correctly	1 1	
4	it reflects light	1	
5 a	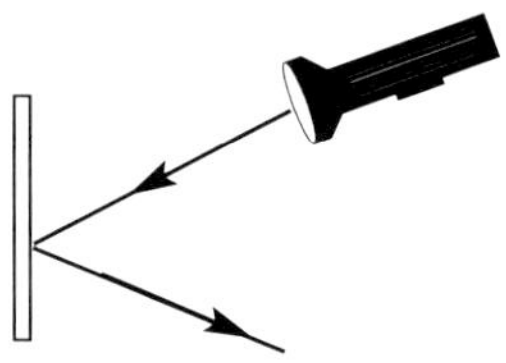 arrow from torch to mirror arrow from mirror	1 1	accept approximately correct direction for each arrow
b	bounces off is turned by, blocks	1	both correct for 1 mark

6F 3	How we see things			Mark
1	how does the distance of the object from the light affect the shadow size?	how does the distance of the object from the wall affect the shadow size?	how does the distance of the torch from the object affect the shadow size?	1
2	distance of object from the torch	distance of object from the wall	distance of torch from the object	1
3	**any two from:** same object; same torch; same position of torch; same position of screen/wall	**any two from:** same object; same torch; same position of torch; same position of screen/wall	**any two from:** same object; same torch; same position of object; same position of screen/wall	1 both needed
4	size of shadow, distance of object from wall	size of shadow, distance of object from torch	size of shadow, distance of object from wall	2
5	ruler/metre stick			1
6	do the test again or more than once or check with another group			1
7	the graph will allow him to work out shadow sizes for distances he did not test or allow him to see the pattern of his results			1
8	2 marks for a double comparative, even if the prediction is incorrect, e.g. the closer it is to the wall, the smaller the shadow 1 mark only for a single comparative, e.g. when it is near the wall, it will be small			2
Extra information for questions 1 to 4: 1 accept how does the different angle of light source affect the shadow size? 2 accept angle of light source or angle of light to object 3 **any two from:** same object; same torch; same position of object on floor; same distance 4 accept size of shadow, shape of shadow				

6G 1	Changing circuits	Mark	Extra information
1	B ticked	1	
2 a		1	
b	———	1	
c	it completes or breaks a circuit	1	it turns circuits on or off
3 a	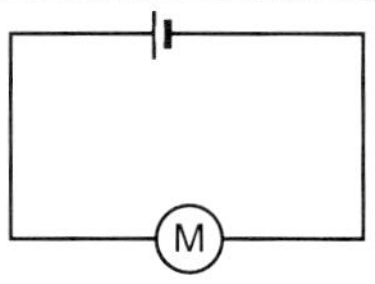	1	allow straight or curved lines for wires; they should touch or almost touch the components
b	add more cells or batteries	1	
4	paper clip and key circled	2	
5	plastic is an insulator or not an electrical conductor so it makes it safe to touch or stops short circuits	1 1	

6G 2	Changing circuits	Mark	Extra information
1	C and D	1	both ticked
2	motor cell/battery switch	2	all three correct 2 marks any two correct 1 mark
3	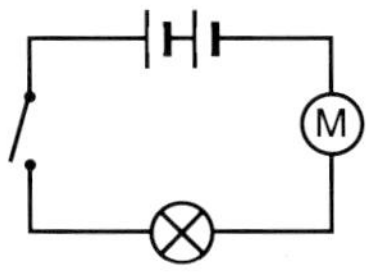	2	international symbols 1 mark joined correctly 1 mark allow parallel circuits
4	provides power or electricity	1	
5	metals	1	
6	mains electricity has a higher voltage or is more powerful and could kill you	1	accept the converse
7	a switch closes to complete or make a circuit or make a bulb light open the switch to break the circuit or stop the electricity flowing or turn off the light	1 1	

6G 3	Changing circuits		Mark
1	does the thickness of the wire affect the brightness of the bulb?	does the length of the wire affect the brightness of the bulb?	1
2	circled wire in three different thicknesses but the same length	circled wire in three different lengths but the same thickness	1
3	thickness of wire	length of wire	1
4	**any two from:** same type (material) of wire; same cells; same bulb; same length of wire; same way to connect	**any two from:** same type (material) of wire; same cells; same bulb; same thickness of wire; same way to connect	2
5	brightness of bulb		1
6	light sensor or brightness scale; accept direct comparison		1
7	do the test again or more than once or check with another group or use a meter to measure the electricity/current		1
8	2 marks for a double comparative even if the prediction is incorrect, e.g. the thicker the wire, the brighter the bulb or the shorter the wire, the brighter the bulb 1 mark only for a single comparative, e.g. if the wire is thick, the bulb is bright		2

Answers and mark schemes for Test 4s

6A 4	Interdependence and adaptation	Mark	Extra information
1 a	they absorb light or they help the plant to make food	1	accept they make food
b	to make her test fair	1	
c	11 cm circled	1	
d	it cannot be 11 cm in week 2 and then shrink to 10 cm in week 3 because plants keep growing	2	the reason gets the second mark accept 10 circled if reason given is that it should be larger as it is growing quickly
e	it has a few leaves or has grown some leaves	1	
f	to check the results of her test or because all the plants might not be/stay healthy or to get reliable results	1	accept any reasonable answer
2 ai	roots do not need to grow deep to anchor the plant because the soil is sticky and heavy;	1	
ii	water is often near the surface because it does not soak easily through clay soil	1	
b	roots must be shown deeper; a tap root could be drawn	1	

6B 4	Micro-organisms	Mark	Extra information
1 a	any two from: same type of strawberries; same aged strawberries; all strawberries washed/wrapped/stored in the same way	2	
b	strawberry with no mould 2°C; strawberry with a little mould 8°C; strawberry with a lot of mould 15°C	1	all three correct 1 mark
c	the colder the temperature, the less mould grows (or the opposite)	2	if it is cold not much mould grows for 1 mark
d	it grows or there are more patches of mould at 15°C	1	accept there is more of it
2	air and water/moisture	1	both correct for the mark
3 a	gas	1	accept carbon dioxide
bi	it grows or is bigger or it reproduces	1	accept it feeds off sugar
ii	it gives off gas	1	accept carbon dioxide given off

6C 4	More about dissolving	Mark	Extra information
1 a	**any two from:** same amount of salt; same amount of water; same place; same environmental conditions; same amount of stirring	2	
b	180 circled	1	
c	he averages the results	1	accept he takes the middle value
d	line lower and can become less steep	1	must not increase
e	the higher the temperature, the quicker it dissolves (or similar)	2	when it is hot it dissolves quickly (or similar) for 1 mark
f	evaporate the water	1	accept boil off the water
2 a	there is a chemical reaction taking place (and new material has been made as a result)	1	accept a reaction or air trapped in the powder
b	gas or air	1	

6D 4	Reversible and irreversible changes	Mark	Extra information
1 a	the amount of bicarbonate of soda	1	
b	**any two from:** same amount of vinegar; same sized/shape bottle; same temperature; same type of vinegar and bicarbonate of soda	2	
c	the balloon will be biggest (for that amount)	1	
d	NO	1	
e	a new material or gas has been made	1	accept you cannot get bicarbonate back by evaporating the solution
2 a	melting	1	
b	freezing or solidifying	1	
c	ice	1	
d	becomes a gas	1	accept boils

6E 4	Forces in action	Mark	Extra information
1 a	**any one from:** same material for parachute; same height drop; same weight used; same method of release	1	
b	the '8' on 20 cm parachute 3rd try circled	1	
c	to check their results or for reliability	1	
d	work out an average	1	accept take the middle value
e	22 seconds	1	unit required
f	the larger the parachute, the longer it takes to fall (or vice versa)	2	big parachutes take a long time to fall (or vice versa) for 1 mark
g	as you move along the parachute axis, the line of the graph goes up	1	accept any reasonable explanation of the trend
h	one arrow upwards labelled air resistance or drag or friction one arrow downwards labelled gravity or weight	1 1	give 1 mark for both arrows of approximately equal size, but no labels

6F 4	How we see things	Mark	Extra information
1 a	a protractor	1	accept angle measurer
b	it is shiny	1	accept it is smooth; do not accept it bounces off
c	24° circled	1	accept 40° circled
d	number in the range 39–41°	1	if 40° circled, 23–25°; unit not required
e	do the test again	1	
f	the angle of reflection is the same size as the angle at which the light hits the mirror	1	accept the angle light bounces off is the same as it hits the mirror
g	arrow drawn pointing away from the mirror at approximately equal angle	1	accept ±10° of correct angle; the arrow must be a straight line
2	Ali	1	
3	one arrow drawn from lamp towards drink	1	arrows must be straight and touch the glass/drink
	one arrow drawn from drink towards Min's eye	1	

6G 4	Changing circuits	Mark	Extra information
1 a	any two from: same type of bulb; same type of wires; same length of wire; same type of cells	2	
b	light sensor or light meter	1	
c	the cross for two cells is at a point higher than for one cell but lower than for three cells	1	
	the cross for 6 cells is on the x axis, i.e. at zero	1	
d	the bulb has burnt out	1	accept 6
e	6V	1	unit required
f	the more cells or voltage, the brighter the bulb until it burns out	2	
2	uppermost bulb circled	1	the bulb in the outer series circuit

Pupil record sheets

Name:	Class:	Date:

Unit 6A: Interdependence and adaptation 1

Qn	Objective	Level	Mark	☺ 😐 ☹
1	Know that plants need light to grow well	3	/1	
2	Give the functions of the root	4	/2	
3a	Know where a plant makes food	5	/1	
3b	State two things a plant uses to make food	5	/1	
4a	Give one way animals use plants	4	/1	
4b	Give one way plants need animals	4	/1	
5	Make a key to sort flowers	4	/3	

Unit 6A: Interdependence and adaptation 2

Qn	Objective	Level	Mark	☺ 😐 ☹
1a	Know that plants need light to make food	5	/1	
1b	Give two other things a plant needs to grow	3	/2	
2	Explain how a polar bear is suited to its environment	3	/2	
3	Give a reason for the use of fertiliser	4	/1	
4a	Put arrows in a food chain	4	/1	
4b	Identify predators and prey	4	/2	
4c	Explain why a food chain needs a plant	5	/1	

Unit 6A: Interdependence and adaptation 3

Qn	Objective	Level	Mark	☺ 😐 ☹
1	Formulate a question to test	5	/1	
2	Select the equipment for a fair test	5	/1	
3	Identify the variable	4	/1	
4	Elements of a fair test	3	/3	
5	Know what must be measured	3	/1	
6	State what must be used for measuring	3	/1	
7	Explain why more than one plant should be used	4	/1	
8	Give a way to present the results	4	/1	

Unit 6A: Interdependence and adaptation 4

Qn	Objective	Level	Mark	☺ 😐 ☹
1a	Leaves make food for plants	5	/1	
1b	Explain why we use plants of the same size and type	3	/1	
1cd	Identify an incorrect measurement and explain	4	/3	
1e	Give difference in plant	3	/1	
1f	Explain why more than one plant should be used	4	/1	
2a	Explain why a plant is suited to clay soil	5	/2	
2b	Draw a plant suited to sandy soil	5	/1	

Name:	Class:	Date:

Unit 6B: Micro-organisms 1

Qn	Objective	Level	Mark	☺😐☹
1a	Know that germs cause disease	4	/1	
1b	Know that germs are too small to see	4	/1	
2	Explain how cleaning your teeth helps prevent decay	5	/2	
3	Give two good uses of micro-organisms	4/5	/2	
4	Give two bad effects of micro-organisms	4/5	/2	
5	Know why cooked and raw foods should be stored separately	5	/2	

Unit 6B: Micro-organisms 2

Qn	Objective	Level	Mark	☺😐☹
1	Give two life processes	2	/2	
2a	Recognise that objects decay	4	/2	
2b	Know that micro-organisms cause decay	5	/1	
3	Know that foods can be produced using micro-organisms	5	/2	
4a	Know what micro-organisms need to grow well	4	/1	
4b	Give two ways to preserve food	5	/2	

Unit 6B: Micro-organisms 3

Qn	Objective	Level	Mark	☺😐☹
1	Formulate a question to test	5	/1	
2	Identify the variable	4	/1	
3	Elements of a fair test	3	/3	
4	Know what must be measured	4	/1	
5	State what must be used for measuring	3	/1	
6	State how to check a test	3	/1	
7	Predict a conclusion	5	/2	

Unit 6B: Micro-organisms 4

Qn	Objective	Level	Mark	☺😐☹
1a	Elements of a fair test	3	/2	
1b	Know that more mould grows at warmer temperatures	4	/1	
1c	Predict a conclusion	4	/2	
1d	Evidence that mould is living	5	/1	
2	Know what micro-organisms need to grow well	4	/1	
3a	Identify bubbles as gas	5	/1	
3b	Identify evidence that yeast is living	5	/2	

Name: Class: Date:

Unit 6C: More about dissolving 1

Qn	Objective	Level	Mark	☺😐☹
1	Identify solutions	4	/2	
2a	Know some solids that dissolve	3	/1	
2b	Know term insoluble	3	/1	
3	Explain why solutions can't be separated with filters	5	/1	
4	Explain how to separate salt, sand and water	5	/3	
5	Explain why rain is not salty	5	/2	

Unit 6C: More about dissolving 2

Qn	Objective	Level	Mark	☺😐☹
1a	Identify solids that dissolve in water	4	/2	
1b	State that a dissolved solid makes a solution	4	/1	
1c	Know that a dissolved solid is still in the water	4	/1	
2a	Explain how to separate a mixture	4	/1	
2b	Explain how the method works	5	/1	
3	Describe how to separate a solution	4/5	/2	
4a	Know condensation results in a liquid	4	/1	
4b	Know the liquid is water from the air	5	/1	

Unit 6C: More about dissolving 3

Qn	Objective	Level	Mark	☺😐☹
1	Formulate a question to test	5	/1	
2	Identify the variable	4	/1	
3	Elements of a fair test	3	/2	
4	Know what must be measured	4	/1	
5	State what must be used for measuring	3	/1	
6	State how to check a test	3	/1	
7	Give a way to record the results	4	/1	
8	Predict a conclusion	5	/2	

Unit 6C: More about dissolving 4

Qn	Objective	Level	Mark	☺😐☹
1a	Elements of a fair test	3	/2	
1b	Identify the incorrect result	4	/1	
1c	Know how to average results	5	/1	
1d	Continue a line graph	4	/1	
1e	Draw a conclusion	4/5	/2	
1f	Getting solid from solution	4	/1	
2a	Recognise a reaction taking place	5	/1	
2b	Identify bubbles as gas	5	/1	

Name:	Class:	Date:

Unit 6D: Reversible and irreversible changes 1

Qn	Objective	Level	Mark	☺😐☹
1	Classify the nature and reversibility of a change	4/5	/5	
2	State that burning is irreversible and give the reason why	3/5	/2	
3	Complete the table for changes when heated	3	/3	

Unit 6D: Reversible and irreversible changes 2

Qn	Objective	Level	Mark	☺😐☹
1	Know safety measures for burning test	4	/3	
2	State that new materials are made when paper burns	5	/2	
3	Identify the materials that burn	3/4	/3	
4	Name changes of state involving solids and liquids	4	/2	

Unit 6D: Reversible and irreversible changes 3

Qn	Objective	Level	Mark	☺😐☹
1	Identify the variable	4	/1	
2	Elements of a fair test	3	/3	
3	Know what must be measured	4	/1	
4	State what must be used for measuring	3	/1	
5	State how to check the test	3	/1	
6	Interpret a line graph	5	/1	
7	Explain how a graph does/does not support a statement	5	/1	
8	Interpret a line graph	4	/1	

Unit 6D: Reversible and irreversible changes 4

Qn	Objective	Level	Mark	☺😐☹
1a	Identify the test variable	4	/1	
1b	Elements of a fair test	3	/2	
1c	Observation of volumes	5	/1	
1de	State if the change is reversible and give the reason why	5	/2	
2ab	Name change of state of solid to liquid and the reverse process	4	/2	
2c	Use the table to show a statement is false	5	/1	
2d	Ice melts and forms water, which then boils	4	/1	

Name: Class: Date:

Unit 6E: Forces in action 1

Qn	Objective	Level	Mark	☺😐☹
1a	Name a forcemeter	3	/1	
1b	Name the units to measure force	3	/1	
2	Identify forces	4	/1	
3	Mark forces on a diagram	5	/2	
4a	Understand that objects weigh less in water	4	/2	
4b	Give a reason why objects weigh less in water	5	/1	
5a	Know that air resistance slows moving objects	4	/1	
5b	Know how to reduce air resistance	4	/1	

Unit 6E: Forces in action 2

Qn	Objective	Level	Mark	☺😐☹
1	Know the direction in which gravity acts	4	/1	
2	Know there is less gravity on the Moon	5	/1	
3	Read a forcemeter and know the units it uses	3	/2	
4	Know the forces acting on an object falling through air	4/5	/3	
5	Know the effect of forces on an object moving through water	5	/3	

Unit 6E: Forces in action 3

Qn	Objective	Level	Mark	☺😐☹
1	Formulate a question to test	5	/1	
2	Select equipment for a fair test	4	/1	
3	Identify the variable	4	/1	
4	Elements of a fair test	3	/2	
5	Know what must be measured	4	/1	
6	State what must be used for measuring	3	/1	
7	State how to check the results	3	/1	
8	Explain why the results need to be checked	4	/1	
9	Give a way to present the results	4	/1	

Unit 6E: Forces in action 4

Qn	Objective	Level	Mark	☺😐☹
1a	Elements of a fair test	3	/1	
1b	Identify an incorrect result	4	/1	
1c	Explain why a test is repeated	3	/1	
1d	Know how to calculate an average result	4	/1	
1e	Read a line graph	5	/1	
1f	Draw a conclusion from a line graph	4/5	/2	
1g	Explain how the graph supports the conclusion	5	/1	
1h	Names of forces	4/5	/2	

Name:	Class:	Date:

Unit 6F: How we see things 1

Qn	Objective	Level	Mark	☺😐☹
1a	Know the direction in which a shadow falls	3	/1	
1b	Know why a shadow is made	4	/1	
2	State that opaque objects make a dark shadow	4	/1	
3a	Draw arrows for the path of light, showing the angle of incidence equals the angle of reflection	5	/2	
3b	Give a way to change the size of a shadow	5	/1	
3c	Draw arrows for seeing an object	5	/2	
4	Know the difference between shadow and reflection	4	/2	

Unit 6F: How we see things 2

Qn	Objective	Level	Mark	☺😐☹
1a	Know that we see when light enters our eyes	5	/1	
1b	Know how a shadow is made	4	/1	
2a	Match the shadow to the object	4	/1	
2b	Describe an object as opaque/transparent/translucent	4	/1	
3	Draw arrows for seeing an object	5	/2	
4	Explain why precious stones are shiny	4	/1	
5a	Draw arrows for seeing an object in a mirror	5	/2	
5b	Know the difference between shadow and reflection	4	/1	

Unit 6F: How we see things 3

Qn	Objective	Level	Mark	☺😐☹
1	Formulate a question to test	5	/1	
2	Identify the variable	4	/1	
3	Elements of a fair test	3	/1	
4	Know what must be measured	4	/2	
5	State what must be used for measuring	3	/1	
6	State how to check a test	3	/1	
7	Explain that a line graph is a good choice for the results	5	/1	
8	Predict a conclusion	5	/2	

Unit 6F: How we see things 4

Qn	Objective	Level	Mark	☺😐☹
1a	Select equipment to measure angles	4	/1	
1b	Explain why a mirror reflects light	3	/1	
1c	Identify an incorrect measurement	4	/1	
1d	Use pattern to correct the measurement	4	/1	
1e	State how a test can be checked	3	/1	
1f	Describe what the results show	4	/1	
1g	Reflection of light ray	5	/1	
2	Largest shadows formed by objects nearest light source	5	/1	
3	Drawing a reflected ray of light	5	/2	

Name:	Class:	Date:

Unit 6G: Changing circuits 1

Qn	Objective	Level	Mark	☺😐☹
1	Identify complete circuits	3	/1	
2ab	Know the symbols for components	4	/2	
2c	Describe the function of a switch	4	/1	
3a	Draw a circuit diagram using symbols	5	/1	
3b	Give a way to change the speed of a motor	5	/1	
4	Identify electrical conductors	4	/2	
5	Explain why electrical wires have a plastic coating	4/5	/2	

Unit 6G: Changing circuits 2

Qn	Objective	Level	Mark	☺😐☹
1	Identify complete circuits	3	/1	
2	Know the symbols for components	4	/2	
3	Draw a circuit with specified components	4/5	/2	
4	Know the function of a cell	4	/1	
5	Give a material that conducts electricity	4	/1	
6	Explain why batteries are safe but mains electricity isn't	4	/1	
7	Describe how a switch works	4/5	/2	

Unit 6G: Changing circuits 3

Qn	Objective	Level	Mark	☺😐☹
1	Formulate a question to test	5	/1	
2	Select equipment for a fair test	3	/1	
3	Identify the variable	4	/1	
4	Elements of a fair test	3	/2	
5	Know what must be measured	4	/1	
6	State what must be used for measuring	3	/1	
7	State how to check a test	3	/1	
8	Predict a conclusion	5	/2	

Unit 6G: Changing circuits 4

Qn	Objective	Level	Mark	☺😐☹
1a	Elements of a fair test	3	/2	
1b	Give equipment to measure brightness	4	/1	
1c	Fill in missing measurements	4	/2	
1d	Explain why five batteries give no light	4	/1	
1e	Interpret a graph	5	/1	
1f	Draw a conclusion	5	/2	
2	Completing a circuit	5	/1	

The marks and level thresholds for Year 6

Mark ranges for sub-levels for all six summative Test 4s (end-of-year tests)								
3c	3b	3a	4c	4b	4a	5c	5b	5a
4–9	10–18	19–24	25–31	32–40	41–46	47–53	54–62	63–70

Topic A Interdependence and adaptation

NC level	Test 1	Test 2	Test 3	Test 4
3	1	4	5	2
4	7	4	3	4
5	2	2	2	4

Overall mark ranges for sub-levels for Tests 1–4								
Mark ranges for sub-levels for Test 1 (prior learning)								
3c	3b	3a	4c	4b	4a	5c	5b	5a
2	2	3	4	5	6	7	8	9–10
Mark ranges for sub-levels for Test 2 (knowledge and understanding)								
3c	3b	3a	4c	4b	4a	5c	5b	5a
3	3	4	5	6	7	8	9	10
Mark ranges for sub-levels for Test 3 (mainly Sc1)								
3c	3b	3a	4c	4b	4a	5c	5b	5a
3	3	4	5	6	7	8	9	10
Mark ranges for sub-levels for Test 4 (part of end-of-year summative Test 4s)								
3c	3b	3a	4c	4b	4a	5c	5b	5a
2	2	3	4	5	6	7	8	9–10

Mark ranges for sub-levels for summative Tests 2 and 3								
3c	3b	3a	4c	4b	4a	5c	5b	5a
5	6–7	8–9	10–11	12–13	14–15	16	17–18	19–20

Topic B Micro-organisms

NC level	Test 1	Test 2	Test 3	Test 4
3	0	2	5	2
4	4	3	2	4
5	6	5	3	4

Overall mark ranges for sub-levels for Tests 1-4								
Mark ranges for sub-levels for Test 1 (prior learning)								
3c	3b	3a	4c	4b	4a	5c	5b	5a
N/A	1	2	3	3	4	5–6	7–8	9–10
Mark ranges for sub-levels for Test 2 (knowledge and understanding)								
3c	3b	3a	4c	4b	4a	5c	5b	5a
2	2	3	4	4	5	6	7–8	9–10
Mark ranges for sub-levels for Test 3 (mainly Sc1)								
3c	3b	3a	4c	4b	4a	5c	5b	5a
2	2	3	4	5	6–7	8	9	10
Mark ranges for sub-levels for Test 4 (part of end-of-year summative Test 4s)								
3c	3b	3a	4c	4b	4a	5c	5b	5a
2	2	3	4	5	6	7	8	9–10

Mark ranges for sub-levels for summative Tests 2 and 3								
3c	3b	3a	4c	4b	4a	5c	5b	5a
5	6	7–8	9	10–11	12–13	14–15	16–17	18–20

Topic C More about dissolving

NC level	Test 1	Test 2	Test 3	Test 4
3	2	0	4	2
4	2	7	3	4
5	6	3	3	4

Overall mark ranges for sub-levels for Tests 1-4								
Mark ranges for sub-levels for Test 1 (prior learning)								
3c	3b	3a	4c	4b	4a	5c	5b	5a
1	2	3	4	4	5	6	7–8	9–10
Mark ranges for sub-levels for Test 2 (knowledge and understanding)								
3c	3b	3a	4c	4b	4a	5c	5b	5a
2	2	3	4	4	5	6	7–8	9–10
Mark ranges for sub-levels for Test 3 (mainly Sc1)								
3c	3b	3a	4c	4b	4a	5c	5b	5a
2	2	3–4	5	6	7	8	9	10
Mark ranges for sub-levels for Test 4 (part of end-of-year summative Test 4s)								
3c	3b	3a	4c	4b	4a	5c	5b	5a
2	2	3	4	5	6	7	8	9–10

Mark ranges for sub-levels for summative Tests 2 and 3								
3c	3b	3a	4c	4b	4a	5c	5b	5a
4	5	6–7	8–9	10–11	12–13	14–15	16–17	18–20

Topic D Reversible and irreversible changes

NC level	Test 1	Test 2	Test 3	Test 4
3	4	1	5	2
4	3	7	3	4
5	3	2	2	4

Overall mark ranges for sub-levels for Tests 1-4								
Mark ranges for sub-levels for Test 1 (prior learning)								
3c	3b	3a	4c	4b	4a	5c	5b	5a
2	3	4	5	6	7	8	9	10
Mark ranges for sub-levels for Test 2 (knowledge and understanding)								
3c	3b	3a	4c	4b	4a	5c	5b	5a
2	2	3	4	5	6	7	8	9–10
Mark ranges for sub-levels for Test 3 (mainly Sc1)								
3c	3b	3a	4c	4b	4a	5c	5b	5a
3	3	4	5	6	7	8	9	10
Mark ranges for sub-levels for Test 4 (part of end-of-year summative Test 4s)								
3c	3b	3a	4c	4b	4a	5c	5b	5a
2	2	3	4	5	6	7	8	9–10

Mark ranges for sub-levels for summative Tests 2 and 3								
3c	3b	3a	4c	4b	4a	5c	5b	5a
5	6	7–8	9–10	11–12	13–14	15–16	17–18	19–20

Topic E Forces in action

NC level	Test 1	Test 2	Test 3	Test 4
3	2	2	4	2
4	5	3	5	4
5	3	5	1	4

Overall mark ranges for sub-levels for Tests 1-4								
Mark ranges for sub-levels for Test 1 (prior learning)								
3c	3b	3a	4c	4b	4a	5c	5b	5a
2	2	3	4	5	6	7	8	9–10
Mark ranges for sub-levels for Test 2 (knowledge and understanding)								
3c	3b	3a	4c	4b	4a	5c	5b	5a
2	2	3	4	4	5	6	7–8	9–10
Mark ranges for sub-levels for Test 3 (mainly Sc1)								
3c	3b	3a	4c	4b	4a	5c	5b	5a
3	3	4	5	6	7	8	9	10
Mark ranges for sub-levels for Test 4 (part of end-of-year summative Test 4s)								
3c	3b	3a	4c	4b	4a	5c	5b	5a
2	2	3	4	5	6	7	8	9–10

Mark ranges for sub-levels for summative Tests 2 and 3								
3c	3b	3a	4c	4b	4a	5c	5b	5a
4	5–6	7–8	9	10–11	12–13	14–15	16–17	18–20

Topic F How we see things

NC level	Test 1	Test 2	Test 3	Test 4
3	1	0	3	2
4	4	5	3	4
5	5	5	4	4

Overall mark ranges for sub-levels for Tests 1–4								
Mark ranges for sub-levels for Test 1 (prior learning)								
3c	3b	3a	4c	4b	4a	5c	5b	5a
1	2	3	4	4	5	6	7–8	9–10
Mark ranges for sub-levels for Test 2 (knowledge and understanding)								
3c	3b	3a	4c	4b	4a	5c	5b	5a
1	2	3	4	4	5	6	7–8	9–10
Mark ranges for sub-levels for Test 3 (mainly Sc1)								
3c	3b	3a	4c	4b	4a	5c	5b	5a
2	2	3	4	5	6	7	8	9–10
Mark ranges for sub-levels for Test 4 (part of end-of-year summative Test 4s)								
3c	3b	3a	4c	4b	4a	5c	5b	5a
2	2	3	4	5	6	7	8	9–10

Mark ranges for sub-levels for summative Tests 2 and 3								
3c	3b	3a	4c	4b	4a	5c	5b	5a
3	4–5	6–7	8	9–10	11–12	13–14	15–17	18–20

Topic G Changing circuits

NC level	Test 1	Test 2	Test 3	Test 4
3	1	1	5	2
4	6	7	2	4
5	3	2	3	4

Overall mark ranges for sub-levels for Tests 1–4								
Mark ranges for sub-levels for Test 1 (prior learning)								
3c	3b	3a	4c	4b	4a	5c	5b	5a
2	2	3	4	5	6	7	8	9–10
Mark ranges for sub-levels for Test 2 (knowledge and understanding)								
3c	3b	3a	4c	4b	4a	5c	5b	5a
2	2	3	4	5	6	7	8	9–10
Mark ranges for sub-levels for Test 3 (mainly Sc1)								
3c	3b	3a	4c	4b	4a	5c	5b	5a
3	3	4	5	6	7	8	9	10
Mark ranges for sub-levels for Test 4 (part of end-of-year summative Test 4s)								
3c	3b	3a	4c	4b	4a	5c	5b	5a
2	2	3	4	5	6	7	8	9–10

Mark ranges for sub-levels for summative Tests 2 and 3								
3c	3b	3a	4c	4b	4a	5c	5b	5a
4	5–6	7–8	9–10	11–12	13–14	15–16	17–18	19–20

Reliability and predictions

The first and most critical step in producing high-quality tests is to ensure that each question addresses the part of the topic that has been taught. Equally importantly, a reliable level needs to be attributed to every mark. Finally, every test must cover the content of the topic in a fair and balanced manner. That is, it should contain some easy, some medium and some hard questions. It is then possible to work out a set of theoretical pass mark thresholds and these are discussed below. Theory and practice must come together, however, and the Rising Stars tests need to be standardised and linked to the National Curriculum levels established by QCA for the tests to be reliable and valid. These equated sub-levels are given on pages 65–68.

Standardising the tests

Rising Stars conducted research with a sample of schools in April, May and June 2008. Pupils sat a number of the end-of-year tests in science (i.e. the Test 4s) of the topics they had been taught that year. The scores the pupils obtained on each test were used to generate an overall score – equivalent to taking all six end-of-year tests for the year.

In Year 6, the Rising Stars combined Test 4s score was standardised by equating to the results the pupils obtained in the KS2 national tests.

In other years, the standardisation process involved averaging sub-levels obtained from the QCA optional tests in mathematics, reading and writing and equating to them. (In Year 1, this was teacher assessment.)

This method was chosen to provide an externally validated test-based comparison for the levels. In addition, a check was made in each year of the average science teacher assessment to this average level from the optional tests. See the Appendix for further details. There is a strong similarity, but as all teachers know, some children are more talented at science than English or mathematics. This difference will be highlighted by the teacher's own assessment, which draws on a wider range of information and evidence.

The table below summarises the number of schools and pupils that undertook to participate in the research.

Year	1	2	3	4	5	6
Number of pupils	238	256	303	301	386	483
Number of schools	8	9	8	7	8	10

Some of the schools were unable to complete the research or could only provide partial data. Consequently, final sample was approximately one third of the above numbers in each year.

In addition to providing test scores, teachers and pupils in the schools also commented on the language, illustrations and suitability of the questions in the tests. A number of the questions were refined and improved thanks to this advice.

The equating data for the end-of-year tests

The raw scores from the schools for the end-of-year tests (Test 4s) were collated together and equated to the average of the sub-levels as described below and reported by the schools for the relevant year. These standardising exercises were undertaken by an independent specialist, who for many years undertook similar work for QCA.

Standardisation of tests – technical information

The equating data was used to validate an algorithm that could then be applied to Tests 1, 2 and 3. This algorithm is shown below. The algorithm works on the understanding that pupils will do better on easier questions and score less well on harder ones.

- Questions at their working level – pupils get correct 50% of the marks available;
- Questions at one level *below* their working level – pupils get correct 70% of the marks available;
- Questions at two levels *below* their working level – pupils get correct all of the marks available;
- Questions at one level *above* their working level – pupils are able to get correct 20% of the marks available;
- Questions at two levels *above* their working level – are too hard for pupils and they get correct none of the marks available.

By applying the above algorithm to the test scores, they can be translated into a consistent set of indicative levels and sub-levels from a standardised theoretical base.

A word of warning

Level threshold information is provided for all tests, but it is recommended that at least two tests – e.g. Tests 2 and 3 – be used to ensure there is sufficient coverage and balance for a valid and reliable summative level for the topic.

Appendix

Comparison of science levels and the average of reading, writing and mathematics

The table below is a comparison of the average science TA sub-levels with the average sub-level of reading, writing and mathematics obtained from the QCA optional tests in Years 2 to 5 and between KS2 levels in Year 6. The sub-levels are expressed as decimals as follows:

- sub-level **a** being worth 0.7;
- sub-level **b** being worth 0.3;
- sub level **c** being the whole number for the level.

There is close agreement between the two sets of averages. The pattern also shows a steady increase in levels from Year 1 to Year 6, as might be expected. Note that the level for Year 1 is close to 2. This suggests rapid progress in Year 1 or pupils now start school with a significant amount of prior learning.

Year	Average science TA sub-level	Average English and mathematics sub-level
1	1.84	1.80
2	2.08	2.08
3	2.98	2.87
4	3.25	3.06
5	3.99	4.03
6	4.59	4.48

Percentiles and standard scores for end-of-year science Test 4s

The standard score and percentile table below shows the distribution of marks and provides relative information about a pupil's performance against his or her year group. Standard scores greater than 115 are well above average, while those less than 85 are well below average.

Standard score	70	80	85	90	100	110	115	120	130
Percentile	2%	9%	16%	26%	50%	74%	84%	91%	98%
End-of-year test score (out of 60 marks)	9	15	19	25	38	50	57	62	68

This combined end-of-year Test 4s has a very strong correlation of pupils' levels with their average KS2 scores from mathematics, reading and writing, giving Pearson's r= 0.76. There is also a very strong correlation of pupils' science KS2 levels with their test score giving Pearson's r= 0.72. There is a reasonably good correlation between pupils' ages and their test score, giving Pearson's r=0.44.

Overall, the tests have a number of fairly easy marks. They also contain a significant proportion of demanding marks, however, which enable the tests to differentiate able pupils.

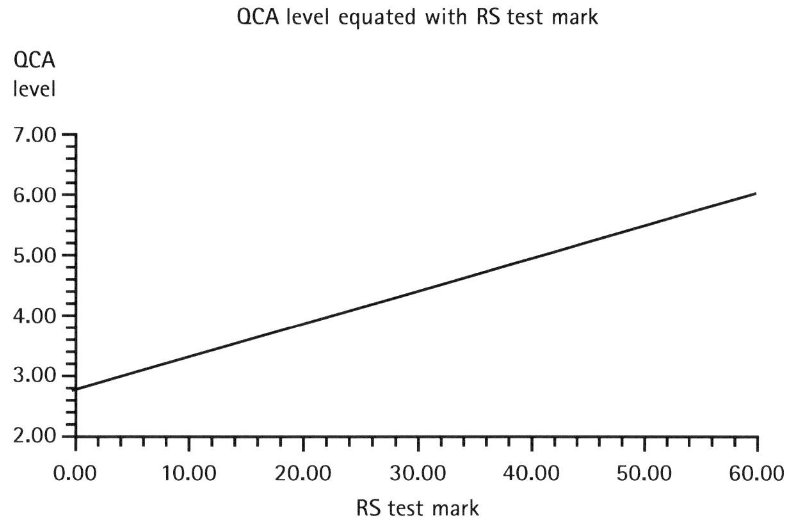